OLD TESTAMENT QUOTATIONS
in the
NEW TESTAMENT

Helps for Translators

UBS Handbook Series:

A Handbook on . . .

Genesis
Exodus
Leviticus
The Book of Joshua
The Book of Ruth
The Book of Esther
The Book of Job
Psalms
Ecclesiastes
Song of Songs
Lamentations
The Book of Daniel
The Book of Amos
The Books of Obadiah, Jonah, and
  Micah
The Books of Nahum, Habakkuk,
  and Zephaniah
The Gospel of Matthew
The Gospel of Mark
The Gospel of Luke
The Gospel of John
The Acts of the Apostles

Paul's Letter to the Romans
Paul's First Letter to the Corin-
  thians
Paul's Second Letter to the Corin-
  thians
Paul's Letter to the Galatians
Paul's Letter to the Ephesians
Paul's Letter to the Philippians
Paul's Letters to the Colossians
  and to Philemon
Paul's Letters to the Thessalo-
  nians
Paul's Letters to Timothy and to
  Titus
The Letter to the Hebrews
The Letter from James
The First Letter from Peter
The Letter from Jude and the Sec-
  ond Letter from Peter
The Letters of John
The Revelation to John

Technical Helps:

Bible Index
Fauna and Flora of the Bible
Greek-English Lexicon of the New
  Testament
Marginal Notes for the Old Testa-
  ment
Marginal Notes for the New
  Testament

New Testament Index
Old Testament Quotations in the
  New Testament
The Practice of Translating
Short Bible Reference System
The Theory and Practice of Trans-
  lation

Old Testament Quotations in the New Testament

by Robert G. Bratcher

UBS Technical Helps Series

UNITED
BIBLE
SOCIETIES

New York

PRINTED IN THE UNITED STATES OF AMERICA

Books in the series of Helps for Translators may be ordered from a national Bible Society or from either of the following centers:

United Bible Societies
European Production Fund
Postfach 81 03 40
70520 Stuttgart
Germany

United Bible Societies
1865 Broadway
New York, NY 10023
U. S. A.

L.C. Cataloging-in-Publication Data

Bible. N.T. English. Selections. 1987
    Old Testament quotations in the New Testament / edited by Robert G. Bratcher in cooperation with the Sub-committee on Translation of the United Bible Societies. — 3rd rev. ed.
       p. cm. — (Helps for translators)
    Includes index
    ISBN 0-8267-0031-4
    1. Bible. O.T.—Quotations in the New Testament. 2. Bible—Translating. 3. Bible. N.T.—Relation to the Old Testament. I. Bratcher, Robert G. II. United Bible Societies. Committee on Translations. III. Bible. O.T. English. Selections. 1987. IV. Title. V. Series.
BS2387.B54 1987
225.5'2046—dc19

                                        87-18632
                                           CIP

ABS-3/06-150-4,150-QWD 12 - 102739

Contents

Introduction

The present list of Old Testament quotations in the New Testament is designed to assist translators in the preservation of the right relationship between such quotations and their Old Testament sources. The problem of the way in which the writers handled the Old Testament is a complex one, and one which it is really not the translator's task to unravel. In translating the Old Testament, the purpose is to reflect as accurately as possible the sense which the Old Testament originals conveyed to their readers; and in translating the New Testament, including the quotations contained therein, one must strive for an accurate representation of what the New Testament writings meant to their readers. It is not the business of the translator to "correct" the New Testament by introducing, for example, a translation from the Hebrew Masoretic Text if the New Testament writer followed the Septuagint or some other rendering.

On the other hand, the present check list should help the translator to make the Old and New Testament materials agree in translation wherever they are truly parallel in their respective originals. In this regard, the use of this list is analogous to the use of the Synopsis of the Four Gospels, in which the translator endeavors to have the translation of the different Gospel passages in substantial agreement when they are the same or closely similar in the different Gospel passages, and to preserve with equal faithfulness the differences between the same accounts. In terms of the Gospel parallels, the ideal is to have verbal identity in the translation when there is verbal identity in the originals, although the translator is encouraged not to extend such identity to the point of an artificial and wooden type of parallelism. But in the Old and New Testament parallels, exact verbal identity of the quotation with its Hebrew source is of course not the ideal in the same sense as in the Gospel passages, for the reason that such identity never existed in the first place—because of the simple fact that the original passage was in Hebrew and the quotation in Greek, with the consequent shades of difference in meaning which are inevitable in any process of translation.

At the same time, it is desirable to strive for general meaning equivalents between the Old and New Testament passages insofar as they are parallel. A study of the corresponding Old Testament passages to determine what was the meaning conveyed to their readers, or more especially to the readers of the New Testament times (whether in the Hebrew form or in the Septuagint translation as the case may be) will better enable the New Testament translator to produce a rendering of the quotations in terms of their meaning to the New Testament readers and writers.

This list of Old Testament (OT) quotations in the New Testament (NT) includes all formal quotations and some of the more obvious paraphrases and allusions which seem to reflect a conscious use of a specific Old Testament passage or of Old Testament phraseology. Paraphrases are indicated by (P) immediately following the NT chapter and verse citation of the passage, and allusions by (A). Naturally there will be differences of opinion over the exact number of such allusions: the present list has made use of the earlier compilation issued by the American Bible Society, plus the Greek texts of Westcott and Hort, Nestle, Merk, and BFBS 2nd edition (1958). Other works consulted include C. H. Toy, Quotations in the New Testament, and H. B. Swete, An Introduction to the Old Testament in Greek (pp. 381-405).

This list is not meant to be a model for translation. For the sake of uniformity the text of the English Revised Version of 1881 (ERV) is used (except, very rarely, where otherwise noted) in citing the New Testament passages and the Hebrew Old Testament passages. Only exceptionally are alternate translations given, even when found in the margin of ERV. Translators will naturally avail themselves of other helps and translations in making their own translation. The ERV was chosen because of its literalness in following the Hebrew and Greek originals, its high degree of consistency in employing the same English word in translating a given Hebrew or Greek word, and its differentiation between the singular and plural forms of the second person pronoun by the use of "thou," "thee," and "you," "ye."

The NT passages are in the left hand column and the OT passages in the right hand column. Where the text allows, a poetic structure is employed (largely following ERV) to allow for a quicker and surer comparison between the two columns. In the NT column only the words of the actual quotation itself, or paraphrase, or allusion, are reproduced, without the introductory words. In the OT column only the relevant clauses and words are given; an incomplete citation is identified by ellipsis marks (. . .) either at the beginning or end of the passage.

The chapter and verse identification of the Masoretic Text of an OT passage always conforms to the English version (even where, as frequently in the Psalms, the verse division of Kittel's Masoretic Text differs from that of the English version); the chapter and verse identification of the Septuagint follows the edition of Rahlfs. Where the LXX and MT differ from each other (particularly in the Psalms and Jeremiah), both are given.

Where the NT citation follows the Masoretic Text (MT) of the OT, the ERV translation of the OT passage is given (cf. Jeremiah 31.15 opposite Matthew 2.18). The Septuagint version (LXX) of the OT is cited only in those cases where it differs from the MT and it seems clear that the NT citation follows the LXX and not the MT of the Old Testament (cf. Isaiah 40.3 opposite Matthew 3.3). In such cases the LXX has been translated in the language and style of the ERV, approximating, as much as the Greek text of the LXX allows, the very wording of the ERV translation of the Greek text of the NT. The LXX text here employed is the 4th edition of Alfred Rahlfs (1950). In the cases where the source of the NT quotation is the LXX and not the MT, the MT, in its ERV translation, is cited immediately following its LXX equivalent, so as to allow the translator to ascertain accurately and conveniently (1) wherein the LXX and the MT differ from each other and (2) wherein the NT quotation differs from the MT of the OT.

No account is taken of the LXX: (1) where it agrees with the MT; and (2) where it disagrees with the MT, but it seems clear that the NT citation conforms to the MT and not to the LXX.

The footnotes are meant to make the translator aware of some further problems in connection with the correspondence between the NT quotation and its OT source.

A solid line underscoring a passage indicates that the words underlined have no equivalents in the opposite column (cf. line 2 of Matthew 2.6, and its opposite under Micah 5.2; and Jeremiah 31.15, line 4 and its opposite under Matthew 2.18). A passage printed in italics indicates that the words in italics have their equivalents in the opposite column, but that these do not correspond in all respects (cf. "they shall call" in Matthew 1.23 and "thou shalt call" in LXX Isaiah 7.14).

It is hoped that the format of this compilation will prove practical to the translator in checking the OT source of the NT quotation. Any suggestions or questions will be gratefully received.

Besides the English Revised Version the following English versions are occasionally referred to: King James, 1611 (AV); American Standard Version, 1901 (ASV); Revised Standard Version, 1952 (RSV); The Holy Scriptures of the Jewish Publication Society of America, 1917 (JPS).

Finally we want to acknowledge our debt of gratitude to the American Bible Society for sponsoring this publication, and especially to Dr. Robert G. Bratcher for bearing the main burden of its preparation.

United Bible Societies
Subcommittee on Translation

Introduction to the Second Revised Edition

The UBS Greek New Testament, third corrected edition, contains a revised index of quotations of Old Testament passages. The list in this edition of <u>Old Testament Quotations in the New Testament</u> has been adjusted to reflect some of these revisions. Certain minor corrections and adjustments have been made as well.

We owe our gratitude to Harold P. Scanlin and W. Gerald Kendrick for their careful work in revising the material.

Introduction to the Third Edition

Translators working through the Old Testament frequently find it useful to see how certain passages are quoted in the New Testament. While working on the Haitian Bible, the Rev. Roger Desir compiled a list of the references dealt with in this volume, but arranged according to their sequence in the Old Testament. We are most grateful to him for supplying this list, and it has been added as an appendix in this edition.

Abbreviations

Hebrew Transcription

The following is the system used in this book:

Consonants

א	- '	ל	- l
ב	- b	מ	- m
ג	- g	נ	- n
ד	- d	ס	- s
ה	- h (initial)	ע	- '
ה	- (h) (end of syllable)	פ	- p
ו	- w	צ	- s̩
ז	- z	ק	- q
ח	- ḥ	ר	- r
ט	- ṭ	שׂ	- ś
י	- y (initial)	שׁ	- š
י	- (y) (end of syllable)	ת	- t
כ	- k		

Vowels

◌ָ = ā		Example:	yāda'
◌ַ = a			yāda'
◌ֲ = ă			'ănī
◌ֵ = ē			yēšēb
◌ֶ = e			melek
◌ֱ = ĕ			'ĕlōhīm
◌ְ = e			lᵉ (vocal shewa)
◌ְ = no transliteration			mal'ākīm (silent shewa)
◌ִי = ī			šᵉlīšī
◌ִ = i			higgīd
◌ֹ = or וֹ = ō			kōl
◌ָ = o			kol
◌ֳ = ŏ			ḥŏlī
וּ = ū			šūb
◌ֻ = u			huggad
◌ֵי = ē(y)			bᵉnē(y)
◌ָיו = ā(y)w			bᵉnā(y)w

Matthew

Matthew	Old Testament

Matthew

Old Testament

1.23
Behold, the virgin shall be with child, and shall
bring forth a son, and *they shall call* his name
Immanuel.

LXX Isa 7.14
Behold, the virgin[1] shall be with child, and
shall bring forth a son, and *thou shalt call* his
name Immanuel.

MT
Behold, a *young woman*[2] shall conceive, and
bear a son, and *shall call* his name Immanuel.

2.6
And thou, Bethlehem, *land of Judah*,
Art in no wise least among *the princes* of
    Judah:
For out of thee shall come forth a *governor*,
Which shall be shepherd of my people Israel.[3]

Mic 5.2
But thou, Bethlehem *Ephrathah*,
Which art little to be among *the thousands* of
    Judah,
Out of thee shall one come forth unto me
That is to be *ruler* in Israel.

2.15
Out of Egypt did I call my son.

Hos 11.1
. . . and called my son out of Egypt.

2.18
A voice was heard in Ramah,
Weeping and great mourning,
Rachel weeping for her children;
And she would not be comforted, because they
    are not.

Jer 31.15
. . . A voice is heard in Ramah,
Lamentation, and bitter weeping,
Rachel weeping for her children;
She refuseth to be comforted for her children,
    because they are not.

2.23
He should be called a Nazarene.

No O.T. passage.[4]

3.3 (Mk 1.3; Lk 3.4; Jn 1.23)
The voice of one crying in the wilderness,

LXX Isa 40.3
The voice of one crying in the wilderness,

---

[1] Gk. parthenos, like Mt. 1.23.
[2] RSV. The Heb. 'almāh is translated "virgin" in ERV and "young woman" in RSV. For a study of
the subject cf. TBT July 1958, pp. 97-126.
[3] "Which shall be shepherd of my people Israel": cf. LXX 2 Sam 5.2, "You will be shepherd of my
people Israel."
[4] Perhaps the N.T. Nazōraios alludes to nazir "Nazirite" (cf. Judg 13.5-7); or to nēṣer "branch"
(cf. Isa 11.1) and ṣemaḥ "sprout" (cf. Isa 4.2; Jer 23.5; 33.15). Commentators are not agreed.

Make ye ready the way of the Lord,
Make *his* paths straight.

Make ye ready the way of the Lord,
Make straight the paths *of our God.*

MT
The voice of one that crieth,
Prepare ye in the wilderness the way of the
    Lord,
Make straight <u>in the desert</u> a highway *for our
    God.*

3.17 (A) (17.5; Mk 1.11; 9.7; Lk 3.22; 9.35)
This is my beloved Son, in whom I am well
    pleased.

Psa 2.7: Thou art my son; this day have I
    begotten thee.
Gen 22.2: . . . thine only[5] son, whom thou
    lovest . . .
Isa 42.1: . . . my chosen, in whom my soul
    delighteth.

4.4 (Lk 4.4)
Man shall not live by bread alone, but by every
word that proceedeth out of the mouth of God.

LXX Deut 8.3
Man shall not live by bread alone, but by every
word[6] that proceedeth out of the mouth of
God <u>shall man live.</u>

MT
Man *doth not live* by bread only, but by every
thing[6] that proceedeth out of the mouth of *the
Lord* <u>doth man live.</u>

4.6 (Lk 4.10-11)
He shall give his angels charge concerning
    thee:
<u>And</u> on their hands they shall bear thee up,
<u>Lest</u> haply thou dash thy foot against a stone.

LXX Psa 90.11-12
He shall give his angels charge concerning
    thee . . .
On their hands they shall bear thee up,
Lest haply thou dash thy foot against a stone.

MT Psa 91.11-12
For he shall give his angels charge *over*
    thee . . .
They shall bear thee up in their hands,
Lest thou dash thy foot against a stone.

4.7 (Lk 4.12)
Thou shalt not tempt[7] the Lord thy God.

LXX Deut 6.16
Thou shalt not tempt the Lord thy God.

MT
Ye shall not tempt the Lord *your* God.

---

[5] Heb. et-y^eḥī d^eka: LXX <u>ton agapēton</u> "the beloved"; in certain contexts the Gk. <u>ho agapētos</u>
means "only."
[6] "Word" or "thing": Gk. <u>rēma</u>; the Heb. <u>mōṣā'</u> may mean "thing" or "utterance" (cf. Koehler).
[7] "Tempt": ASV "make trial of."

4.10 (Lk 4.8)
Thou shalt *worship* the Lord thy God,
And him <u>only</u> shalt thou serve.

Deut 6.13
Thou shalt *fear* the Lord thy God; and him
shalt thou serve . . .

4.15-16
The land of Zebulun and the land of Naphtali,
Toward the sea, beyond Jordan,
Galilee of the Gentiles,
The people which *sat* in darkness saw a great
    light,
The people that *walked* in darkness have seen
    a great light:
They that *dwelt* in the land <u>of</u> the shadow of
    death,
Upon them hath the light *shined.*

Isa 9.1-2
In the former time he brought into <u>contempt</u>
    <u>the land of Zebulun and the land of</u>
    Naphtali,
<u>But in the latter time hath he made it glori-</u>
    <u>ous,</u> by the way of the sea, beyond Jor-
    dan,
Galilee of the nations.

And to them which *sat* in the region *and*
    shadow of death,
To them did light *spring up.*

5.5 (A)
<u>Blessed are</u> the meek: <u>for</u> they shall inherit
<u>the earth.</u>[8]

Psa 37.11
But the meek shall inherit the land[8] . . .

**5.21 (19.18; Mk 10.19; Lk 18.20; Rom 13.9; Jas
    2.11)**
Thou shalt not kill.[9]

Exo 20.13 (Deut 5.17)

Thou shalt do no murder.

**5.27 (19.18; Mk 10.19; Lk 18.20; Rom 13.9; Jas
    2.11)**
Thou shalt not commit adultery.

Exo 20.14 (Deut 5.18)

Thou shalt not commit adultery.

5.31 (P) (cf. 19.7)
Whosoever shall put away his wife, let him
give her a writing of divorcement.

Deut 24.1
When a man taketh a wife, and marrieth her,
then it shall be . . . that he shall write her a
bill of divorcement, and give it in her hand,
and send her out of his house.

5.33 (P)
Thou shalt not forswear thyself, but shalt
perform <u>unto the Lord</u> thine oaths.

Lev 19.12: And ye shall not swear by my name
    falsely . . .
Num 30.2: When a man . . . sweareth an oath .
    . . he shall do according to all that
    proceedeth out of his mouth. (cf. Deut
    23.21)

---

[8] Both the Gk. ḡe and the Heb. ʾereṣ may mean "earth," "land," or "country."
[9] "Kill": the Gk. phoneuō may also mean "to murder."

Matthew

5.34-35 (A)
... the heaven ... is the throne of God ...
... the earth ... is the footstool of his
    feet ...
Jerusalem ... is the city of the great King.

Isa 66.1
The heaven is my throne, and the earth is my
    footstool ...
Psa 48.2
... the city of the great King.

5.38
An eye for an eye, and a tooth for a tooth.

Exo 21.24 (Lev 24.20; Deut 19.21)
... eye for eye, tooth for tooth ...

5.43 (19.19; 22.39; Mk 12.31; Lk 10.27; Rom
    13.9; Gal 5.14; Jas 2.8)
Thou shalt love thy neighbor, and hate thine
enemy.

Lev 19.18

... thou shalt love thy neighbor as thyself ...

7.23 (A)
... Depart from me, ye that work iniquity.

Psa 6.8
Depart from me, all ye workers of iniquity ...

8.17
Himself took our *infirmities*, and bare our
diseases.

Isa 53.4
Surely he hath borne our *griefs*,[10] and carried
our *sorrows* ...[11]

9.13
I desire mercy, and not sacrifice.

Hos 6.6
For I desire mercy[12] and not sacrifice ...

10.35-36 (A)
For I came to set a man at variance against
his father, and the daughter against her
mother, and the daughter-in-law against her
mother-in-law: and a man's foes shall be they
of his own household.

Mic 7.6
For the son dishonoureth the father, the
daughter riseth up against her mother, the
daughter-in-law against her mother-in-law; a
man's enemies are the men of his own house.

11.5 (A)
... The blind receive their sight ...
... the poor have good tidings preached to
    them.

Isa 61.1
... to preach good tidings unto the
    meek[13] ...
... the opening of the prison[14] to them that
    are bound.

---

[10] Or "sicknesses": Heb. ḥŏlāyēnū.
[11] Or "pains": Heb. makʾōbēynu.
[12] ASV "goodness"; RSV "steadfast love": Heb. ḥesed.
[13] "Meek": RSV "afflicted"; JPS "humble": Heb. ʿānāwīm.
[14] Or "the opening of the eyes" (JPS; RSV footnote): Heb pᵉqaḥ-qōaḥ (cf. Koehler).

[4]

11.10 (Mk 1.2; Lk 7.27; cf. Mt 3.3)
Behold I send my messenger <u>before thy face,</u>[15]
Who shall prepare *thy* way before *thee.*

Mal 3.1
Behold, I send my messenger, and he shall
prepare *the* way before *me.*

11.23 (A)
. . . shalt thou be exalted unto heaven? thou
shalt go down unto Hades . . .

Isa 14.13, 15
. . . I will ascend into heaven . . . thou shalt be
brought down to Sheol . . .

11.29 (A)
. . . and ye shall find rest *unto* your souls.

Jer 6.16
. . . and ye shall find rest *for* your souls.

12.7 (cf. 9.13)
I desire mercy, and not sacrifice.

Hos 6.6
For I desire mercy and not sacrifice . . .

12.18-21
Behold, my servant whom *I have chosen*;
My *beloved* in whom my soul is well pleased:
I will put my Spirit upon him,
And he shall *declare* judgement to the Gen-
    tiles.
He shall not *strive*, nor cry aloud
Neither shall any one hear his voice in the
    streets.
A bruised reed shall he not break,
And smoking flax shall he not quench,
Till he send forth judgement unto *victory.*

And *in* his name shall the Gentiles hope.

Isa 42.1-3
Behold my servant, whom *I uphold*;
My *chosen*, in whom my soul delighteth:
I have put my spirit upon him;
He shall *bring forth* judgement to the Gentiles.
He shall not *cry*, not lift up,
Nor cause his voice to be heard in the street.
A bruised reed shall he not break.
And the smoking flax shall he not quench:
he shall bring forth judgement in *truth.*

LXX Isa 42.4
And *on* his name shall the Gentiles hope.

MT
And the isles shall wait for his law.

12.40 (A)
. . . Jonah was three days and three nights in
the belly of the whale . . .

Jonah 1.17
. . . Jonah was in the belly of the fish three
days and three nights.

13.14-15 (Mk 4.12; Lk 8.10; Jn 12.40; Acts
    28.26-27)
By hearing ye shall hear, and shall in no wise
    understand;
And seeing ye shall see, and shall in no wise
    perceive:
For this people's heart is waxed gross,

LXX Isa 6.9-10
By hearing ye shall hear, and shall in no wise
    understand;
And seeing ye shall see, and shall in no wise
    perceive:
For this people's heart is waxed gross,
And their ears are dull of hearing,

---

[15] Cf. LXX Exo 23.20: "Behold, I send my messenger before thy face."

[5]

And their ears are dull of hearing,
And their eyes they have closed;
Lest haply they should perceive with their
    eyes,
And hear with their ears,
And understand with their heart,
And should turn again,
And I should heal them.

And their eyes they have closed;
Lest haply they should perceive with their
    eyes,
And hear with their ears,
And understand with their heart,
And should turn again,
And I should heal them.

MT
Hear ye indeed, but understand not; and see ye
indeed, but perceive not.
Make the heart of this people fat,
and make their ears heavy,
and shut their eyes;
lest they see with their eyes,
and hear with their ears,
and understand with their heart,
and turn again
and *be healed.*[16]

13.35
I will open my mouth in *parables*;
I will utter things hidden *from the foundation*
    of the world.[17]

Psa 78.2
I will open my mouth in *a parable*;
I will utter dark sayings *of* old.

15.4a (19.19; Mk 7.10; 10.19; Lk 18.20; Eph
    6.2-3)
Honour thy father and thy mother.

Ex. 20.12 (Deut 5.16)
Honour thy father and thy mother.

15.4b (Mk 7.10)
He that speaketh evil of father or mother, *let*
him die the death.

LXX Exo 21.17
He that speaketh evil of his father, or his
mother, *shall die* the death.

MT
And he that *curseth* his father, or his mother,
shall surely *be put to death.*

15.8-9 (Mk 7.6-7)
This people honoureth me with their lips;
But their heart is far from me.
But in vain do they worship me.

LXX Isa 29.13
This people draws near to me, with their lips
    they honour me,
But their heart is far from me.
But in vain do they worship me,

---

[16] Isa 6.9 in the MT is a command to the people, hence the 2nd person pl. imper.; Isa 6.10 in the
MT is in the form of a command to the prophet, hence the 2nd person sg. imper.; in the LXX and
NT the passage is predictive and declarative.
[17] "The foundation of the world": in Gk. apo katabolēs "from the foundation" without kosmou
"of the world" (which is omitted by a number of early mss. and versions and by most of the modern Greek texts); cf. Arndt & Gingrich katabolē.

Teaching *as* their doctrines the precepts of men.

Teaching the precepts of men *and* doctrines.

MT
Forasmuch as this people draw nigh unto me,
and with their mouth
and with their lips do honour me,
But have removed their heart far from me,
And their fear of me is a commandment of
men which hath been taught them.

16.27 (A) (cf. Rom 2.6; 2 Tim 4.14)
... he shall render unto every man according his deeds.

LXX Psa 61.13 (cf. Prov 24.12)
For thou renderest to every man according to his works.

MT Psa 62.12
For thou renderest to every man according to his work.

17.5 (A) (cf. 3.17)
This is my beloved Son, in whom I am well pleased; hear ye him.

Psa 2.7
Thou art my son: this day have I begotten thee.
Gen 22.2
... thine only[18] son, whom thou lovest ...
Isa 42.1
... my chosen, in whom my soul delighteth ...
Deut 18.15
... unto him ye shall hearken.

18.16 (A) (Jn 8.17; 2 Cor 13.1)
... that at the mouth of two witnesses or three every word[19] *may* be established.

LXX Deut 19.15
... At the mouth of two witnesses *and* at the mouth of three witnesses every word[19] *shall* be established.

MT
At the mouth of two witnesses, or at the mouth of three witnesses, shall a matter[19] be established.

19.4 (P) (Mk 10.6)
... he which made them from the beginning made them male and female.

LXX Gen 1.27 (cf. 5.2)
... male and female he made them.

MT
Male and female created he them.

---

[18] Heb. et-y^eḥī d^ekā: LXX ton agapēton "the beloved." The Gk. ho agapētos, in certain contexts, means "only."
[19] "Word" or "matter": Gk. rēma; Heb. dābār.

[7]

Matthew

19.5 (Mk 10.7-8; 1 Cor 6.16; Eph 5.31)
For this cause shall a man leave his father and mother, and shall cleave to his wife; and the twain shall become one flesh.

LXX Gen 2.24
For this cause shall a man leave his father and his mother, and shall cleave to his wife; and the twain shall become one flesh.

MT
Therefore shall a man leave his father and his mother, and shall cleave unto his wife; and *they* shall be one flesh.

19.7 (P) (cf. 5.31)
... to give a bill of divorcement, and to put her away.

Deut 24.1
... he shall write her a bill of divorcement, and give it in her hand, and send her out of his house.

19.18-19 (cf. 5.21, 27, 43)
Thou shalt not kill.[20] Thou shalt not commit adultery. Thou shalt not steal. Thou shalt not bear false witness. Honour thy father and thy mother; and Thou shalt love thy neighbor as thyself.

Exo 20.12-16; Lev 19.18 (Deut 5.16-20)
Honour thy father and thy mother . . . Thou shalt do no murder. Thou shalt not commit adultery. Thou shalt not steal. Thou shalt not bear false witness against thy neighbor.
. . . Thou shalt love thy neighbour as thyself.

21.5 (Jn 12.15)
Tell ye the daughter of Zion,
Behold, thy King cometh unto thee,
Meek, and riding upon an ass,
And upon a colt the foal of an ass.

Isa 62.11 and Zech 9.9
... Say ye to the daughter of Zion ...
... Behold, thy king cometh unto thee:
He is just and having salvation;[21]
Lowly, and riding upon an ass,
Even upon a colt the foal of an ass.

21.9 (A) (23.39; Mk 11.9; Lk 13.35; 19.38; Jn 12.13)
Hosanna[22] to the Son of David:
Blessed is he that cometh in the name of the Lord;
Hosanna[23] in the highest.

Psa 118.25-26
Save now, we beseech thee, O Lord . . .
Blessed be he that cometh in the name of the Lord . . .

21.13a (Mk 11.7; Lk 19.46)
My house shall be called a house of prayer ...

Isa 56.7b
... For mine house shall be called an house of prayer for all peoples.

---

[20] "Kill": The Gk. phoneuō may also mean "to murder."
[21] Or "He is triumphant and victorious" (RSV, JPS); LXX "he is just and saving."
[22] Gk. ōsanna = Heb. hōšī'ā(h)nā' "save now"; the LXX, unlike the NT, translates the Heb. by sōson dē "save now."
[23] Ibid.

[8]

21.13b (A) (cf. Mk 11.17) . . . but ye make it a den of robbers.	Jer 7.11 Is this house, which is called by my name, become a den of robbers in your eyes?

21.16 Out of the mouth of babes and sucklings thou hast perfected praise.	LXX Psa 8.3 Out of the mouth of babes and sucklings thou hast perfected praise. MT Psa 8.2 Out of the mouth of babes and sucklings *hast thou established strength.*

21.33 (A) . . . A man . . . planted a vineyard, and set a hedge about it,[24] and digged a winepress in it, and built a tower . . .	Isa 5.1-2 My well-beloved had a vineyard . . . and he made a trench about it, and gathered out the stones thereof, and planted it with the choic- est vine, and built a tower in the midst of it, and also hewed out a winepress therein . . .

21.42 (Mk 12.10-11; Lk 20.17; Acts 4.11; 1 Pet 2.7) The stone which the builders rejected, The same was made the head of the corner: This was from the Lord, And it is marvelous in our eyes.	Psa 118.22-23 The stone which the builders rejected Is become the head of the corner. This is the Lord's doing;[25] It is marvelous in our eyes.

22.24 (P) (Mk 12.19; Lk 20.28) If a man die, having no children, his brother shall marry[26] his wife, and raise up seed unto his brother.[27]	Deut 25.5 If brethren dwell together, and one of them die, and have no son, the wife of the dead shall not marry without unto a stranger: her hus- band's brother shall go in unto her, and take her to him to wife, and perform the duty of an husband's brother unto her.

22.32 (Mk 12.26; Lk 20.37; Acts 7.32) I am the God of Abraham, and the God of Isaac, and the God of Jacob.	Ex 3.6 (cf. 3.15) I am the God of thy father, the God of Abra- ham, the God of Isaac, and the God of Jacob.

---

[24] "And set a hedge about it"; cf. LXX kai phragmon perietheka kai echarakōsa "and I set a
hedge about it and fenced it" (Isa 5.2).
[25] Heb. "this (is) from the Lord."
[26] "Marry": Gk. epigambreusei "he shall perform the duty of a husband's brother toward," equivalent to the Hebrew yābam in Deut 25.5. LXX has gambreuō in Gen 38.8, but not here.
[27] "And raise up seed unto his brother": cf. Gen 38.8b.

Matthew

22.37 (Mk 12.29-30; Lk 10.27)
Thou shalt love the Lord thy God with all thy heart, and with all thy soul, and with all thy *mind*.

Deut 6.5
Thou shalt love the Lord thy God with all thine heart, and with all thy soul, and with all thy *might*.

22.39 (cf. 19.19)
Thou shalt love thy neighbor as thyself.

Lev 19.18
Thou shalt love thy neighbor as thyself.

22.44 (Mk 12.36; Lk 20.42-43; Acts 2.34-35; 1 Cor 15.25; Heb 1.13)
The Lord *said* unto my Lord,
Sit thou on my right hand,
Till I put thine enemies *underneath*[28] thy feet.

LXX Psa 109.1
The Lord said unto my lord,
Sit thou on my right hand,
Till I put thine enemies *as a footstool of* thy feet.

MT Psa 110.1
The Lord *saith*[29] unto my lord,
Sit thou at my right hand,
Until I make thine enemies thy *footstool*.

23.38 (A) (Lk 13.35)
. . . your house is left unto you desolate.

Jer 22.5
. . . this house shall become a desolation.

23.39 (A) (cf. 21.9)
Blessed is he that cometh in the name of the Lord

Psa 118.26
Blessed be he that cometh in the name of the Lord . . .

24.15 (A) (Mk 13.14)
. . . the abomination of desolation . . .

Dan 11.31 (12.11)
. . . they shall set up the abomination that maketh desolate.[30]

24.30b (A) (Mk 13.26; Lk 21.27)
. . . the Son of man coming on the clouds of heaven . . .

LXX Dan 7.13
. . . and on the clouds of heaven there came one like a son of man . . .

MT
There came with the clouds of heaven one like unto a son of man.

---

[28] "Underneath thy feet": cf. Psa 8.6b.

[29] There is no tense indicated in the Heb. nᵉ'um "utterance."

[30] Heb. "the abomination that maketh desolate" is rendered by the LXX "the abomination of desolation": this ambiguous Gk. phrase is probably identical in meaning with the Heb. phrase it translates.

26.15 (A)
. . . And they weighed unto him thirty pieces of silver.

Zech 11.12
. . . So they weighed for my hire thirty pieces of silver.

26.31 (Mk 14.27)
I will *smite* the shepherd, and the sheep <u>of the flock</u> shall be scattered abroad.

Zech 13.7
Smite the shepherd, and the sheep shall be scattered.

26.64 (A) (cf. 22.44; 24.30b)
. . . the Son of man sitting at the right hand of power, and coming on the clouds of heaven.

Psa 110.1 and LXX Dan 7.13
. . . Sit thou at my right hand . . .
. . . and on the clouds of heaven there came one like a son of man . . .

27.9-10
And *they took* the thirty pieces of silver, the price of him that was priced, whom certain of the children of Israel did price; and they gave them for *the potter's field, as the Lord appointed me.*

Zech 11.12-13[31]
So they weighed for <u>my hire</u> thirty pieces of silver.
And the Lord said unto me, <u>Cast it unto the potter,</u>[32] the goodly price that I was priced at of them. And *I took* the thirty pieces of silver, and cast them unto *the potter,* <u>in the house of the Lord.</u>

27.35 (A)
. . . they parted his garments among them, casting lots.

Psa 22.18
They part my garments among them,
And upon my vesture do they cast lots.

27.46 (Mk 15.34)
. . . My God, my God, why hast thou forsaken me?

Psa 22.1
My God, my God, why hast thou forsaken me?

27.48 (A)
. . . vinegar . . . (he) gave him to drink.

Psa 69.21
. . . And in my thirst they gave me vinegar to drink.

---

[31] For this scripture, which the evangelist attributes to Jeremiah and quotes in an altered form, cf. the commentaries, and see TBT July 1958, pp. 121-122.
[32] "Potter": or "treasury" (RSV, JPS). Heb <u>hayōṣēr</u> is "potter," <u>ha'ōṣar</u> "treasury"; LXX has <u>chōneutērion</u> "smelter's furnace."

Mark

Mark	Old Testament

1.2-3 (cf. Mt 11.10; 3.3)
Behold I send my messenger <u>before thy face,</u>[1]
Who shall prepare *thy* way;
 	
The voice of one crying in the wilderness,
Make ye ready the way of the Lord,
Make *his* paths straight.
	Mal 3.1 and LXX Isa 40.3
	Behold, I send my messenger,
	and he shall prepare *the* way <u>before me.</u>
	
	The voice of one crying in the wilderness,
	Make ye ready the way of the Lord,
	Make straight the paths *of our God.*
	
	MT Isa 40.3
	The voice of one that crieth,
	Prepare ye in the wilderness the way of the
	    Lord.
	Make straight <u>in the desert</u> a highway *for our*
	    God.

1.11 (A) (cf. Mt 3.17) Thou art my beloved son, in thee I am well pleased.	**Psa 2.7** Thou art my son, this day have I begotten thee. **Gen 22.2** . . . thine only[2] son, whom thou lovest . . . **Isa 42.1** . . . my chosen, in whom my soul delight- eth . . .

4.12 (Mt 13.14-15)
That seeing they may see, and not perceive;
and hearing they may hear, and not under-
stand; lest haply they should turn again, *and it*
should be forgiven them.
	LXX Isa 6.9-10
	By hearing ye shall hear, and shall in no wise
	    understand;
	And seeing ye shall see, and shall in no wise
	    perceive . . .
	
	Lest haply . . . they should turn again,
	and I should heal them.
	
	MT
	Hear ye indeed, but understand not;
	and see ye indeed, but perceive not . . .[3]
	Lest they . . . turn again, *and be healed.*

---

[1] Cf. LXX Exo 23.20: "Behold, I send my messenger before thy face."

[2] Heb <u>et-y^eḥî d^ekā</u>: LXX <u>ton agapēton</u> "the beloved"; in certain contexts the Gk. <u>ho agapētos</u> means "only."

[3] The passage in the MT is in the form of a command to the people, hence the 2nd person pl. imper.; in the LXX and NT the passage is predictive.

4.29 (A)
. . . he putteth forth the sickle, because the harvest is come.

LXX Joel 3.13
Send ye out the sickle, for the harvest is come.

MT
Put ye in the sickle, for the harvest is ripe.

6.34 (A)
. . . they were as sheep not having a shepherd.

Num 27.17 (cf. 1 Kgs 22.17; Ezek 34.5)
. . . that the congregation of the Lord be not as sheep which have no shepherd.

7.6 7 (cf. Mt 15.8-9)
This people honoureth me with their lips,
But their heart is far from me.
But in vain do they worship me,
Teaching *as* their doctrines the precepts of men.

LXX Isa 29.13
This people draws near to me, with their lips they honour me,
But their heart is far from me.
But in vain do they worship me,
Teaching the precepts of men *and* doctrines.

MT
Forasmuch as this people draw nigh unto me, and with their mouth and with their lips do honour me,
But have removed their heart far from me,
And their fear of me is a commandment of men which hath been taught them.

7.10a (cf. Mt 15.4a)
Honour thy father and thy mother.

Exo 20.12 (Deut 5.16)
Honour thy father and thy mother.

7.10b (cf. Mt 15.4b)
He that speaketh evil of father or mother, *let him die* the death.

LXX Exo 21.17
He that speaketh evil of *his* father or *his* mother, *shall die* the death.

MT
And he that *curseth* his father, or his mother, shall surely *be put to death.*

8.18 (A)
Having eyes see ye not? and having ears, hear ye not?

Jer 5.21 (cf. Ezek 12.2)
O foolish people . . . which have eyes, and see not; which have ears, and hear not.

9.7 (A) (cf. Mt 17.5)
This is my beloved Son: hear ye him.

Psa 2.7
Thou art my son: this day have I begotten thee.
Gen 22.2
. . . thine only[4] son, whom thou lovest . . .

[13]

Deut 18.15
. . . unto him ye shall hearken.

9.48 (A)
. . . where their worm dieth not, and the fire is not quenched.

Isa 66.24
. . . for their worm shall not die, neither shall their fire be quenched.

10.4 (P) (cf. Mt 19.7)
. . . to write a bill of divorcement, and to put her away.

Deut 24.1
. . . he shall write her a bill of divorcement . . . and send her out of his house.

10.6 (P) (cf. Mt 19.4)
. . . male and female made he them.

LXX Gen 1.27 (cf. 5.2)
. . . male and female he made them.

MT
Male and female created he them.

10.7-8 (cf. Mt 19.5)
For this cause shall a man leave his father and mother, and shall cleave to his wife,[5] and the twain shall become one flesh . . .

LXX Gen 2.24
For this cause shall a man leave his father and *his* mother, and shall cleave to his wife; and the twain shall become one flesh.

MT
Therefore shall a man leave his father and his mother, and shall cleave unto his wife: and *they* shall be one flesh.

10.19 (cf. Mt 19.18-19)
Do not kill.[6] Do not commit adultery. Do not steal. Do not bear false witness.[7] Do not defraud. Honour thy father and mother.

Exo 20.12-16
Honour thy father and thy mother . . . Thou shalt do no murder. Thou shalt not commit adultery. Thou shalt not steal. Thou shalt not bear false witness against thy neighbor.

---

[4] Heb. et-y^e̱ḥīd^eḵā: LXX ton agapēton "the beloved." In certain contexts the Gk. ho agapētos means "only."

[5] "And shall cleave to his wife" is included by Textus Receptus, Souter, Soden, Vogels, and Merk; omitted by Westcott and Hort, Tischendorf, Nestle, Lagrange, and Taylor.

[6] "Kill": the Gk. phoneuō may also mean "to murder."

[7] ERV translates here the four negative commands "Do not . . ." and in Mt 19.18 "Thou shalt not . . . ." The Greek text in Mt employs ou with the fut. ind. of the verb (as does the LXX of Exo 20.13-16), while in Mk (and Lk 18.20) it employs mē with the 1st aor. subj. of the verb. There is no difference in meaning between the two forms of the negative command, and the ERV distinction seems oversubtle.

11.9-10 (A) (cf. Mt 21.9)
Hosanna;[8] Blessed is he that cometh in the
name of the Lord . . . Hosanna[8] in the highest.

Psa 118.25-26
Save now, we beseech thee, O Lord . . .
Blessed be he that cometh in the name of the
Lord . . .

11.17a (cf. Mt 21.13a)
My house shall be called a house of prayer for
all the nations.

Isa 56.7b
. . . For mine house shall be called an house of
prayer for all peoples.

11.17b (A) (cf. Mt 21.13b)
. . . but ye have made it a den of robbers.

Jer 7.11
Is this house, which is called by my name,
become a den of robbers in your eyes?

12.1 (A) (cf. Mt 21.33)
A man planted a vineyard, and set a hedge
about it,[9] and digged a pit for the winepress,
and built a tower . . .

Isa 5.1-2
My well-beloved had a vineyard . . . and he
made a trench about it, and gathered out the
stones thereof, and planted it with the choic-
est vine, and built a tower in the midst of it,
and also hewed out a winepress therein . . .

12.10-11 (cf. Mt 21.42)
The stone which the builders rejected,
The same was made the head of the corner:
This was from the Lord,
And it is marvelous in our eyes.

Psa 118.22-23
The stone which the builders rejected
Is become the head of the corner.
This is the Lord's doing;[10]
It is marvelous in our eyes.

12.19 (P) (cf. Mt 22.24)
If a man's brother die, and leave a wife behind
him and leave no child, that his brother should
take his wife,[11] and raise up seed unto his
brother.[12]

Deut 25.5
If brethren dwell together, and one of them
die, and have no son, the wife of the dead shall
not marry without unto a stranger: her husband's brother shall go in unto her, and take
her to him to wife, and perform the duty of an
husband's brother unto her.

---

[8] Gk. ōsanna = Heb. hōšī'ā(h)nā, "save now"; the LXX, unlike the NT, translates the Heb. by
sōson dē "save now."

[9] "And set a hedge about it": cf. LXX kai phragmon periethēka kai echarakōsa "and I set a
hedge about it and fenced it" (Isa 5.2).

[10] Heb. "this (is) from the Lord."

[11] Mk resembles the LXX translation of Deut 25.5 more closely than does Mt 22.24. Mk has
labē . . . ton gunaika "he should take the wife" (LXX kai lēmpsetai autēn heautō gunaika "and
he shall take her to himself as wife"), whereas Mt has epigambreusei "he will perform the duty
of a husband's brother" in conformity with the Hebrew expression.

[12] "And raise up seed unto his brother": cf. Gen 38.8b.

12.26 (cf. Mt 22.32)
I am the God of Abraham, and the God of
Isaac, and the God of Jacob.

Exo 3.6 (cf. 3.15)
I am the God of thy father, the God of Abraham, the God of Isaac, and the God of Jacob.

12.29-30 (cf. Mt 22.37)
Hear, O Israel; The Lord our God, the Lord is
one; and thou shalt love the Lord thy God with
all thy heart, and with all thy soul, and with
all thy mind, and with all thy strength.

Deut 6.4-5
Hear, O Israel: the Lord our God is one Lord:
and thou shalt love the Lord thy God with all
thine heart, and with all thy soul, and with all
thy might.[13]

12.31 (cf. Mt 22.39)
Thou shalt love thy neighbor as thyself.

Lev 19.18
Thou shalt love thy neighbor as thyself.

12.32-33 (P) (cf. 12.29-31)
. . . he is one; and there is none other but he:
and to love him with all the heart, and with all
the understanding, and with all the strength,
and to love his neighbor as himself . . .

Deut 6.4-5: see above.
Deut 4.35: . . . there is none else beside him.

Lev 19.18: see above.

12.36 (cf. Mt 22.44)
The Lord *said* unto my Lord,
Sit thou on my right hand,
Till I put thine enemies underneath[14] thy feet.

LXX Psa 109.1
The Lord said unto my lord,
Sit thou on my right hand
Till I put thine enemies *as a footstool of* thy
feet.

MT Psa 110.1
The Lord *saith*[15] unto my lord,
Sit thou at my right hand,
Until I make thine enemies thy footstool.

13.14 (A) (cf. Mt 24.15)
. . . the abomination of desolation . . .

Dan 11.31 (12.11)
. . . they shall set up the abomination that
maketh desolate.[16]

---

[13] "Might": Heb. m$^{e'}$od; LXX translates dunamis; Mk (and Lk) has ischus.

[14] "Underneath" (hupokatō) is read by Westcott and Hort, Nestle, Bible Societies, Lagrange,
Taylor, RSV; hupopodion "footstool" is preferred by Textus Receptus, Tischendorf, Soden,
Souter, Vogels, and Merk.

[15] There is no tense in the Heb. n$^{e'}$um "utterance."

[16] Heb. "the abomination that maketh desolate" is rendered by the LXX "the abomination of
desolation": this ambiguous Gk. phrase is probably identical in meaning with the Heb. phrase it
translates.

13.26 (A) (cf. Mt 24.30b)
. . . the Son of man coming in clouds . . .

Dan 7.13
. . . there came with[17] the clouds of heaven one like unto a son of man . . .

14.27 (cf. Mt 26.31)
I will smite the shepherd, and the sheep shall be scattered abroad.

Zech 13.7
Smite the shepherd, and the sheep shall be scattered.

14.62 (A) (cf. Mt 26.64; Mk 12.36; 13.26)
. . . the Son of man sitting at the right hand of power, and coming with the clouds of heaven.

Psa 110.1 and Dan 7.13

. . . Sit thou at my right hand . . .
. . . there came with the clouds of heaven one like unto a son of man . . .

15.24 (A) (cf. Mt 27.35)
. . and (they) part his garments among them, casting lots upon them . . .

Psa 22.18
They part my garments among them,
And upon my vesture do they cast lots.

15.34 (Mt 27.46)
. . . My God, my God, why hast thou forsaken me?

Psa 22.1
My God, my God, why has thou forsaken me?

15.36 (A) (cf. Mt 27.48)
. . . vinegar . . . (he) gave him to drink.

Psa 69.21
. . . And in my thirst they gave me vinegar to drink.

16.19 (A) (cf. 12.36; 14.62)
. . . (he) sat down at the right hand of God.

Psa 110.1
. . . Sit thou at my right hand . . .

Luke

Luke

1.17 (A)
. . . Elijah, to turn the hearts of the fathers to the children . . .

Mal 4.5-6
Behold, I will send you Elijah . . . and he shall turn the heart of the fathers to the children . . .

----

[17] "With": LXX has <u>epi</u> "on" (as does Mt 24.30b).

Luke

1.48 (A)
For he hath looked upon the low estate of his
handmaiden . . .

LXX 1 Sam 1.11
Do you look upon the low estate of thy handmaiden . . .

MT
If thou wilt indeed look on the affliction of
thine handmaiden . . .

1.50 (A)
And his mercy is unto generations and genera-
    tions
On them that fear him.

Psa 103.17
But the mercy of the Lord is from everlasting
    to everlasting.
Upon them that fear him.

1.76 (A) (cf. Mt 11.10)
Thou shalt go before the Lord to make ready
his ways.

Mal 3.1
I send my messenger, and he shall prepare the
way before me.

1.79 (A) (cf. Mt 4.16)
To shine upon them that sit in darkness and
the shadow of death . . .

Isa 9.2
The people that walked in darkness have seen
a great light: they that dwelt in the land of
the shadow of death, upon them hath the light
shined.

2.23 (P)
Every male that openeth the womb shall be
called holy to the Lord.

Exo 13.2 (cf. 13.12, 15)
Sanctify unto me all the firstborn, whatsoever
openeth the womb.

2.24
A pair of turtledoves, or two young pigeons.

Lev 12.8
. . . She shall take two turtledoves, or two
young pigeons.

2.52 (A)
And Jesus advanced in wisdom and stature,
and in favour with God and men.

1 Sam 2.26
And the child Samuel grew on, and was in
favour both with the Lord, and also with men.

3.4-6 (cf. Mt 3.3)
The voice of one crying in the wilderness,
Make ye ready the way of the Lord,
Make *his* paths straight.
Every valley shall be filled,
And every mountain and hill shall be brought
    low;
And the crooked shall become straight,
And the rough ways *smooth*;
And all flesh shall see the salvation of God.

LXX Isa 40.3-5
The voice of one crying in the wilderness,
Make ye ready the way of the Lord,
Make straight the paths *of our God*.
Every valley shall be filled,
And every mountain and hill shall be brought
    low;
And all the crooked places shall become
    straight,
And the rough way *level*.

[18]

And the glory of the Lord shall appear,
And all flesh shall see the salvation of God.

MT
The voice of one that crieth,
Prepare ye in the wilderness the way of the
      Lord,
Make straight in the desert a highway *for our*
      God.
Every valley shall be *exalted,*
And every mountain and hill shall be made
      low:
And the crooked shall be made straight,
And the rough places *plain*:
And the glory of the Lord shall be revealed,
And all flesh shall see it together.

3.22 (A) (cf. Mt 3.17)
Thou art my beloved Son; with thee I am well
    pleased.

Psa 2.7: Thou art my son; this day have I
    begotten thee.
Gen 22.2: . . . thine only[1] son, whom thou
    lovest . . .
Isa 42.1: . . . my chosen, in whom my soul
    delighteth.

4.4 (cf. Mt 4.4)
Man shall not live by bread alone.

LXX Deut 8.3
Man shall not live by bread alone . . .

MT
Man *doth not live* by bread only . . .

4.8 (cf. Mt 4.10)
Thou shalt *worship* the Lord thy God,
And him only shalt thou serve.

Deut 6.13
Thou shalt *fear* the Lord thy God;
and him shalt thou serve . . .

4.10-11 (cf. Mt 4.6)
He shall give his angels charge concerning
    thee, to guard thee:
and,
On their hands they shall bear thee up,
Lest haply thou dash thy feet against a stone.

LXX Psa 90.11-12
He shall give his angels charge concerning
    thee,
to guard thee in all thy ways,

On their hands they shall bear thee up,
Lest haply thou dash thy foot against a stone.

MT Psa 91.11-12
For he shall give his angels charge over thee,
    to keep thee in all thy ways.

---

[1] Heb. et-y^eḥī d^ekā: LXX ton agapēton "the beloved"; in certain contexts the Gk. ho agapētos
means "only."

They shall bear thee up in their hands,
Lest thou dast thy foot against a stone.

4.12 (cf. Mt 4.7)
Thou shalt not tempt[2] the Lord thy God.

LXX Deut 6.16
Thou[3] shalt not tempt the Lord thy God.

MT
Ye shall not tempt the Lord *your* God.

4.18-19 (cf. Mt 11.5)
The Spirit of the Lord is upon me,
Because he anointed me to preach good tidings
    to the poor:
He hath sent me to proclaim release to the
    captives,
And recovering of sight to the blind,
To set at liberty them that are bruised,[4]
To *proclaim* the acceptable year of the Lord.

LXX Isa 61.1-2 (cf. Isa 58.6)
The Spirit of the Lord is upon me,
Because he anointed me to preach good tidings
    to the poor:
He hath sent me to heal the brokenhearted,[5]
To proclaim release to the captives,
And recovering of sight to the blind,
To *announce* the acceptable year of the
    Lord . . .

MT
The spirit of the Lord God is upon me;
Because *the Lord* hath anointed me to preach
    good tidings unto the meek;
He hath sent me to bind up the brokenhearted,
To proclaim liberty to the captives,
And the opening *of the prison to them that are
    bound*;
To proclaim the acceptable year of the
    Lord . . .

7.22 (A) (cf. 4.18)
The blind receive their sight, the lame walk,
the lepers are cleansed, and the deaf hear, the
dead are raised up, and the poor have good
tidings preached to them.

Isa 35.5-6 and 61.1
Then the eyes of the blind shall be opened,
and the ears of the deaf shall be unstopped.
Then shall the lame man leap as an hart . . .
. . . to preach good tidings unto the meek . . .[6]

7.27 (cf. Mt 11.10)
Behold, I send my messenger before thy face,[7]

Mal 3.1
Behold, I send my messenger,

---

[2] "Tempt": ASV "make trial of."
[3] "Thou" sg. in NT and LXX; MT "ye" pl.
[4] "To set at liberty them that are bruised": cf. LXX Isa 58.6: "Set at liberty them that are bruised."
[5] This punctuation of these two lines in LXX follows the ERV punctuation of the text in Luke; Rahlfs punctuates the LXX text as follows: ". . . because he anointed me; to preach good tidings to the poor he hath sent me, to heal the brokenhearted . . ." (cf. alternate punctuation of the Lucan text in Nestle).
[6] "Meek": RSV "afflicted"; JPS "humble"; Heb. 'anāwīm.

Who shall prepare *thy* way before *thee*.   and he shall prepare *the* way before *me*.

8.10 (A) (cf. Mk 4.12)
... that seeing they may not see, and hearing they may not understand.

LXX Isa 6.9
Hearing ye shall hear, and shall in no wise understand; and seeing ye shall see, and shall in no wise perceive ...

MT
Hear ye indeed, but understand not; and see ye indeed, but perceive not.

9.35 (A) (cf. Mt 17.5)
This is my Son, my chosen; hear ye him!

Psa 2.7: Thou art my son; this day have I begotten thee.
Isa 42.1: ... my chosen, in whom my soul delighteth ...
Deut 18.15: ... unto him ye shall hearken.

9.54 (A)
... Wilt thou that we bid fire to come down from heaven, and consume them?

2 Kgs 1.10 (cf. 1.12)
... Let fire come down from heaven, and consume thee and thy fifty.

10.15 (A) (cf. Mt 11.23)
... shalt thou be exalted unto heaven? thou shalt be brought down unto Hades

Isa 14.13, 15
... I will ascend into heaven ... thou shalt be brought down to Sheol ...

10.27 (cf. Mt 22.37, 39)
Thou shalt love the Lord thy God with all thy heart, and with all thy soul, and with all thy strength, and with all thy mind; and thy neighbor as thyself.

Deut 6.5 and Lev 19.18
Thou shalt love the Lord thy God will all thine heart, and with all thy soul, and with all thy *might*.

Thou shalt love thy neighbor as thyself.

12.53 (A) (cf. Mt 10.35)
They shall be divided, father against son, and son against father; mother against daughter and daughter against her mother; mother-in-law against her daughter-in-law, and daughter-in-law against her mother-in-law.

Mic 7.6
For the son dishonoureth the father, the daughter riseth up against her mother, the daughter-in-law against her mother-in-law ...

---

7 Cf. LXX Exo 23.20: "Behold, I send my messenger before thy face."

Luke

13.27 (A) (cf. Mt 7.23) ... Depart from me, all ye workers of iniquity.	Psa 6.8 Depart from me, all ye workers of iniquity ...

13.35a (A) (cf. Mt 23.38) ... your house is left unto you (desolate).	Jer 22.5 ... this house shall become a desolation.

13.35b (A) (cf. Mt 23.39) Blessed is he that cometh in the name of the Lord.	Psa 118.26 Blessed be he that cometh in the name of the Lord ...

18.20 (cf. Mt 19.18-19) Do not commit adultery. Do not kill.[8] Do not steal. Do not bear false witness. Honour thy father and mother.	Exo 20.12-16 (Deut 5.16-20) Honour thy father and thy mother ... Thou shalt do no murder. Thou shalt not commit adultery. Thou shalt not steal. Thou shalt not bear false witness <u>against thy neighbor.</u>

19.38 (A) (cf. Mt 21.9) Blessed is the King that cometh in the name of the Lord.	Psa 118.26 Blessed be he that cometh in the name of the Lord ...

19.46a (cf. Mt 21.13a) And my house *shall be* a house of prayer ...	Isa 56.7b ... For mine house *shall be called* an house of prayer <u>for all peoples.</u>

19.46b (A) (cf. Mt 21.13b) ... but ye have made it a den of robbers.	Jer 7.11 Is this house, which is called by my name, become a den of robbers in your eyes?

20.9 (A) (cf. Mt 21.33) A man planted a vineyard ...	Isa 5.1-2 My well-beloved had a vineyard ... and (he) planted it with the choicest vine ...

20.17 (cf. Mt 21.42) The stone which the builders rejected, The same was made the head of the corner.	Psa 118.22 The stone which the builders rejected Is become the head of the corner.

---

[8] "Kill": the Gk. <u>phoneuō</u> may also mean "to murder."

20.28 (P) (cf. Mt 22.24)
If a man's brother die, having a wife, and he be childless, his brother should take the wife,[9] and raise up seed unto his brother.[10]

Deut 25.5
If brethren dwell together, and one of them die, and have no son, the wife of the dead shall not marry without unto a stranger: her husband's brother shall go in unto her, and take her to him to wife, and perform the duty of an husband's brother unto her.

20.37 (P) (cf. Mt 22.32)
. . . when he calleth the Lord the God of Abraham, and the God of Isaac, and the God of Jacob.

Exo 3.6 (cf. 3.15)
I am the God of thy father, the God of Abraham, the God of Isaac, and the God of Jacob.

20.42-43 (cf. Mt 22.44)
The Lord *said* unto my Lord,
Sit thou on my right hand,
Till I put thine enemies as a footstool of thy
  feet.

LXX Psa 109.1
The Lord said unto my lord,
Sit thou on my right hand,
Till I put thine enemies as a footstool of thy
  feet.

MT Psa 110.1
The Lord *saith*[11] unto my lord,
Sit thou at my right hand,
Until I make thine enemies thy footstool.

21.27 (A) (cf. Mt 24.30b)
. . . the Son of man coming in a cloud . . .

Dan 7.13
. . . there came *with* the clouds of heaven one like unto a son of man . . .

21.34-35 (A)
. . . as a snare: for so shall it come upon all them that dwell on the face of all the earth.

Isa 24.17
Fear, and the pit, and the snare, are upon thee, O inhabitant of the earth.

22.37
And he was reckoned with transgressors . . .

Isa 53.12
. . . and he was numbered with the transgressors . . .

22.69 (A) (cf. Mt 26.64)
But from henceforth shall the Son of man be seated at the right hand of the power of God.

Psa 110.1
. . . Sit thou at my right hand . . .

----

[9] "His brother should take the wife": the same as in Mk 12.19. Cf. footnote there.
[10] "And raise up seed unto his brother": cf. Gen 38.8b.
[11] There is no tense indicated in the Heb. n$^{e'}$um "utterance."

Luke

23.30 (A)
Then shall they begin to say to the mountains,
Fall on us; and to the hills, Cover us.

Hos 10.8
. . . And thy shall say to the mountains, Cover
us; and to the hills, Fall on us.

23.34 (A) (cf. Mt 27.35)
And parting his garments among them, they
cast lots.

Psa 22.18
They part my garments among them,
And upon my vesture do they cast lots.

23.46 (A)
Father, into thy hands I commend my
spirit . . .

Psa 31.5
Into thine hand I commend my spirit . . .

24.46 (P)
Thus is is written, that the Christ should
suffer, and rise again from the dead the third
day.

No O.T. passage.[12]

John

John

1.23 (cf. Mt 3.3)
I am the voice of one crying in the wilderness,
Make straight the way of the Lord.

Old Testament

LXX Isa 40.3
The voice of one crying in the wilderness,
Make ye ready the way of the Lord,
Make straight the paths of our God.

MT
The voice of one that crieth,
Prepare ye in the wilderness the way of the
        Lord,
Make straight in the desert a highway *for our
        God.*

1.51 (A)
. . . the angels of God ascending and descend-
ing . . .

Gen 28.12
. . . the angels of God ascending and descend-
ing . . .

---

[12] There is no single O.T. passage which speaks specifically of the suffering of the Messiah and
his resurrection from the dead on the third day. The suffering of the Servant of Yahweh is
spoken of in Isaiah 53, and some commentators see in Hosea 6.2 a possible O.T. proof text of the
resurrection on the third day (cf. in Acts 2.25-28 the use of Psa 16.8-11 as scriptural prediction
of the resurrection of Christ).

2.17	Psa 69.9
The zeal of thine house *shall eat* me up.	For the zeal of thine house *hath eaten* me up . . .

6.31 (P)	LXX Psa 77.24 (cf. Exo 16.4, 15; Neh 9.15)
He gave them bread *out of* heaven to eat.	And he rained manna upon them to eat, And he gave them bread *of* heaven.
	MT Psa 78.24
	And he rained down manna upon them to eat. and gave them *of the corn* of heaven.

6.45	LXX Isa 54.13 (cf. Jer 31.33-34)
And they shall all be taught of God.	And all thy sons (shall be) taught of God . . .
	MT
	And all thy children shall be taught *of the Lord* . . .

7.38	No O.T. passage.[2]
. . . Out of his belly shall flow rivers of living water.[1]	

7.42 (P)	Mic 5.2
. . . The Christ cometh of the seed of David,[3] and from Bethlehem, the village where David was.	But thou, Bethlehem Ephrathah . . . out of thee shall one come forth unto me that is to be ruler in Israel . . .

8.17 (cf. Mt 18.16)	Deut 19.15
Yea and in your law it is written, that *the witness of two men* is true.	. . . at *the mouth of two witnesses*, or at the mouth of three witnesses, shall a matter be established.

---

[1] The punctuation here follows RSV (cf. Greek texts of Westcott and Hort, and Nestle), limiting the scriptural quotation to the words "Out of his belly shall flow rivers of living water."

[2] As Toy says, no satisfactory account of the origin of this quotation has yet been given. He himself favors Proverbs 18.4: "The words of a man's mouth are as deep waters; the wellspring of wisdom is as a flowing brook" (the LXX reads "The word in a man's heart is deep water, and a river gushes forth, and a well of life"). Barrett points to Zechariah 14.8, ". . . living waters shall go out from Jerusalem . . ." (cf. also Isa 55.1; 58.11). A most useful study of this passage is provided by E. D. Freed, Old Testament Quotations in the Gospel of John (Leiden: E. J. Brill, 1965), pp. 21-38.

[3] "Of the seed of David": cf. 2 Sam 7.12; Psa 89.3-4.

10.34 I said, Ye are gods.	Psa 82.6 I said, Ye are gods . . .

12.13 (A) (cf. Mt 21.9)
Hosana:[4] Blessed is he that cometh in the
name of the Lord . . .

Psa 118.25-26
Save now, we beseech thee, O Lord . . .
Blessed be he that cometh in the name of the
    Lord . . .

12.15 (cf. Mt 21.5)
Fear not, daughter of Zion:
Behold, thy King cometh,
Sitting on an ass's colt.

Isa 40.9 and Zech 9.9
O thou that tellest good tidings to Zion . . . be
    not afraid . . .
Rejoice greatly, O daughter of Zion . . . behold
    thy king cometh unto thee . . . lowly, and
    riding upon an ass, even upon a colt the
    foal of an ass.

12.34
. . . The Christ abideth for ever . . .

No O.T. passage.[5]

12.38 (Rom 10.16)
Lord, who hath believed our report?
And to whom hath the arm of the Lord been
    revealed?

LXX Isa 53.1
Lord, who hath believed our report?
And to whom hath the arm of the Lord been
    revealed?

MT
Who hath believed our report?
And to whom hath the arm of the Lord been
    revealed?

12.40 (P) (cf. Mt 13.14-15)
He hath blinded their eyes, and he
    hardened their heart,

LXX Isa 6.10[6]
For this people's heart is waxed gross,
    and their ears are dull of hearing,
    and their eyes they have closed;

---

[4] Gk. ōsanna = Heb. hōšī'ā(h)nā' "save now": the LXX, unlike the N.T., translates the Heb. by
sōson dē "save now."
[5] No single O.T. passage conforms to the quotation in John. Commentators point to Psa 89.4-5;
110.4; Isa 9.7; Ezek 37.25; Dan 7.13-14, as possible sources for the idea expressed in the quotation. W.C. van Unnik (Novum Testamentum III, 1959, 174-179) prefers Psa 89.36 (LXX 88.37) as
the source; the LXX reads to sperma autou eis ton aiōna menei "his seed shall abide for ever."
[6] The quotation of Isa 6.10 in Jn 12.40 differs from its quotation in Mt 13.14-15. In Matthew
the quotation agrees with the LXX in registering the verbs in the third person plural of the indicative mode, so that it is the people themselves who perform the actions named; the MT has
the verbs in the second person singular of the imperative mode, so that the prophet is commanded to perform the actions named; in John, by use of third person singular of the indicative
mode, the actions are referred to God.

Lest they should see with their eyes,
    and perceive with their heart,
And should turn,
And I should heal them.

Lest haply they should see with their
    eyes, and hear with their ears, and
    understand with their heart,
And should turn again,
And I should heal them.

MT
Make the heart of this people fat, and
    make their ears heavy, and shut
    their eyes;
Lest they see with their eyes, and hear
    with their ears, and understand
    with their heart,
And turn again,
And be healed.

13.18
He that eateth my bread lifted up his heel
against me.

Psa 41.9
Yea, mine own familiar friend, in whom I
    trusted, which did eat of my bread,
Hath lifted up his heel against me.

15.25
They hated me without a cause.

Psa 69.4 (cf. 35.19)
They that hate me without a cause . . .

19.24 (cf. Mt 27.35)
They parted my garments among them,
And upon my vesture did they cast lots.

LXX Psa 21.19
They parted my garments among them,
And upon my vesture did they cast lots.

MT Psa 22.18
They *part* my garments among them,
And upon my vesture do they *cast* lots.

19.28-29 (A) (cf. Mt 27.48)
. . . I thirst . . . so they put a sponge full of the
vinegar upon hyssop, and brought it to his
mouth.

Psa 69.21
. . . And in my thirst thy gave me vinegar to
drink.

19.36
A bone of him shall not be broken.

Exo 12.46 (cf. Num 9.12; Psa 34.20)
. . . neither shall ye break a bone thereof.

19.37
They shall look on *him* whom they pierced.

Zech 12.10
. . . and they shall look unto *me* whom they
have pierced.

Acts

Acts

Old Testament

1.20a
Let *his* habitation be made desolate,
And let no man dwell *therein* ...

LXX Psa 68.26
Let *their* habitation become desolate,
And let no man dwell *in their tents*.
MT Psa 69.25
Let *their* habitation[1] be desolate;
Let none dwell in their tents.

1.20b
His office let another take.

LXX Psa 108.8
... His office[2] let another take.

MT Psa 109.8
Let another take his *office*.[2]

2.17-21
And it shall be *in the last days,* saith God,
I will pour forth of my Spirit upon all flesh:
And it shall be *after this*
I will pour forth of my Spirit upon all flesh,
And your sons and your daughters shall
      prophesy,
And your young men shall see visions,
And your old men shall dream dreams:
Yea and on my servants and on my hand-
      maidens in those days
Will I pour forth of my Spirit; and they shall
      prophesy.
And I will show wonders in the heaven above,
And signs on the earth beneath;
Blood, and fire, and vapour of smoke:
The sun shall be turned into darkness,
And the moon into blood,
Before the day of the Lord come,
That great and notable day:
And it shall be, that whosoever shall call on
      the name of the Lord shall be saved.

LXX Joel 3.1-5[3]
And your sons and your daughters shall
      prophesy,
And your old men shall dream dreams,
And your young men shall see visions:
And on servants and on handmaidens in those
      days
Will I pour forth of my Spirit.
And I will show wonders in the heaven,
And on the earth;
Blood and fire, and vapour of smoke:
The sun shall be turned into darkness,
And the moon into blood,
Before the day of the Lord come,
That great and notable[4] day:
And it shall be, that whosoever shall call on
      the name of the Lord shall be saved.

MT
And it shall come to pass *afterward,*
That I will pour out my spirit upon all flesh;
And your sons and your daughters shall
      prophesy,
Your old men shall dream dreams,
Your young men shall see visions;

---

[1] "Habitation": the Heb. ṭîrā(h) is "encampment" (Koehler, JPS, ASV fn.); RSV "camp" (cf. commentaries).

[2] "Office": LXX (and Acts) episkopē "overseership"; Heb. pᵉquda(h) "charge" (JPS), "goods" (RSV).

[3] Joel 3.1-5 in LXX and MT: in English Versions, 2.28-32.

[28]

And also upon *the* servants and upon *the*
    handmaidens in those days
Will I pour out my spirit.
And I will show wonders in the heavens *and in*
    the earth,
Blood, and fire, and *pillars* of smoke.
The sun shall be turned into darkness,
And the moon into blood,
Before the great *and terrible*[5] day of the Lord
    come.
And it shall come to pass, that whosoever shall
    call on the name of the Lord shall be
    delivered.

2.25-28
I beheld the Lord always before my face;
For he is on my right hand, that I should not be
    moved:
Therefore my heart was glad, and my tongue
    rejoiced;
Moreover my flesh also shall dwell in hope:
Because thou wilt not leave my soul in Hades,
Neither wilt thou give thy Holy One to see
    corruption.
Thou madest known unto me the ways of life;
Thou shalt make me full of gladness with thy
    countenance.

LXX Psa 15.8-11
I beheld the Lord always before my face;
For he is on my right hand, that I should not be
    moved:
Therefore my heart was glad, and my tongue
    rejoiced;
Moreover my flesh also shall dwell in hope:
Because thou wilt not leave my soul in Hades,
Neither wilt thou give thy Holy One to see
    corruption.
Thou madest known unto me the ways of life;
Thou shalt make me full of gladness with thy
    countenance.

MT Psa 16.8-11
I have set the Lord always before me:
Because he is at my right hand, I shall not be
    moved.
Therefore my heart is glad, and my *glory*
    rejoiceth:
My flesh also shall dwell in *safety.*
For thou wilt not leave my soul to Sheol;
Neither wilt thou *suffer* thine holy one to see
    corruption.
Thou wilt show me the path of life:
In thy presence is fullness of joy;
In thy right hand there are pleasures for
    evermore.

2.30 (P)

. . . God had sworn with an oath to him, that
of the fruit of his loins he would set one upon
his throne.

**Psa 132.11 (cf. Psa 89.3-4; 2 Sam
7.12-13)**
The Lord hath sworn unto David . . . Of the
fruit of thy *body* will I set upon thy throne.

---

[4] "Notable": Gk. epiphanē "glorious," "splendid"; MT has nōrā' "terrible": apparently LXX derived it from rā'ā(h) "to see" instead of from yārē' "to fear."
[5] Ibid.

Acts

2.31 (P) (cf. 2.27)
... neither was he left in Hades, nor did *his flesh* see corruption.

LXX Psa 15.10
... Thou wilt not leave *my soul* in Hades, Neither wilt thou give *thy Holy One* to see corruption.

MT Psa 16.10 (cf. Acts 2.25-28 above)

2.34-35 (cf. Mt 22.44)
The Lord said unto my Lord,
Sit thou on my right hand,
Till I make thine enemies as a footstool of thy feet.

LXX Psa 109.1
The Lord said unto my lord,
Sit thou on my right hand,
Till I put thine enemies as a footstool of thy feet.

MT Psa 110.1
The Lord *saith* unto my lord,
Sit thou at my right hand,
Until I make thine enemies thy footstool.

3.13 (A) (cf. Mt 22.32)
The God of Abraham, and of Isaac, and of Jacob, the God of our fathers . . .

Exo 3.15 (cf. 3.6)
The Lord, the God of your fathers, the God of Abraham, the God of Isaac, and the God of Jacob . . .

3.22-23 (cf. 7.37)
A prophet shall the Lord God raise up unto *you* from among *your* brethren, like unto me;[6] to him shall ye hearken in all things whatsoever he shall speak unto you. And it shall be, that every soul, which shall not hearken to that prophet,[7] shall be utterly destroyed from among *the* people.

LXX Deut 18.15-16 and Lev 23.29
A prophet from among *thy* brethren, like unto me, shall the Lord *thy* God raise up unto *thee*; to him shall ye hearken in all things which you asked from the Lord your God . . . Every soul that shall not be humbled in that day, shall be utterly destroyed from among *his* people.

MT
The Lord *thy* God will raise up unto *thee* a prophet from the midst of thee, of thy brethren, like unto me; unto him ye shall hearken, *according to all that thou desiredst of the Lord thy God* . . . For *whatsoever* soul it be that shall not be afflicted in that same day; he shall be cut off from his people.

3.25 (cf. Gal 3.8)
And in thy seed shall all the *families* of the earth be blessed.

Gen 22.18 (12.3; 26.4; 28.14)
And in[8] thy seed shall all the *nations* of the earth be blessed.[9]

---

[6] "Like unto me": or, connecting hŏs eme with the verb anastēsei, "as he raised me up" (RSV).
[7] Cf. LXX Deut 18.19, "hearken to whatever words the prophet shall speak in my name."
[8] "In thy seed": or "by thy seed" (RSV).
[9] "Shall be blessed": or "shall bless themselves" (ERV fn., RSV).

4.11 (cf. Mt 21.42)	Psa 118.22
He is the stone which was *set at nought* of you the builders, which was made the head of the corner.	The stone which the builders *rejected* Is become the head of the corner.

4.24 (A)	Exo 20.11 (cf. Psa 146.6)
O Lord, thou that didst make the heaven and the earth and the sea, and all that in them is.	. . . The Lord made heaven and earth, the sea, and all that in them is . . .

4.25-26
Why did the Gentiles rage,
And the peoples imagine vain things?
The kings of the earth set themselves in array,
And the rulers were gathered together,
Against the Lord, and against his Anointed.

LXX Psa 2.1-2
Why did the Gentiles rage,
And the peoples imagine vain things?
The kings of the earth set themselves in array,
And the rulers were gathered together,
Against the Lord, and against his Anointed.

MT
Why do the nations rage,
And the peoples imagine *a vain thing*?
The kings of the earth set themselves,
And the rulers *take counsel* together,
Against the Lord, and against his anointed.

7.3	Gen 12.1
Get thee out of thy land, and from thy kindred, and come into the land which I shall shew thee.	Get thee out of thy country, and from thy kindred, and from thy father's house, unto the land that I will shew thee . . .

7.5 (P)	Gen 48.4 (cf. 17.8)
. . . and he promised that he would give it to him in possession, and to his seed after him . . .	Behold, I will make thee, fruitful, and multiply thee, and I will make of thee a company of peoples; and will give this land to thy seed after thee for an everlasting possession.

7.6 (P)	Gen 15.13
. . . that his seed should sojourn in a strange land, and that they should bring them into bondage, and entreat them evil, four hundred years.	Know of a surety that thy seed shall be a stranger in a land that is not theirs, and shall serve them; and they shall afflict them four hundred years.

7.7 (P)	Gen 15.14 and Exo 3.12
And the nation to which they shall be in bondage will I judge, said God: and after that shall they come forth, and serve me in this place.	And also that nation, whom they shall serve, will I judge: and afterward shall they come out . . . . . . when thou hast brought forth the people out of Egypt, ye shall serve God upon this mountain.

7.14 (A)
. . . threescore and fifteen souls.

LXX Gen 46.27 (cf. Exo 1.5)
. . . All the souls of the house of Jacob which came into Egypt were threescore and fifteen.

MT
. . . All the souls of the house of Jacob, which came into Egypt, were *threescore and ten.*

7.18
. . . There arose another king over Egypt, which knew not Joseph.

LXX Exo 1.8
And there arose another king over Egypt, which knew not Joseph.

MT
Now there arose a *new* king over Egypt, which knew not Joseph.

7.27-29 (P)
But he that did his neighbor wrong thrust him away, saying, Who made thee a ruler and a judge over us? Wouldest thou kill me, as thou killedst the Egyptian yesterday? And Moses fled at this saying, and became a sojourner in the land of Midian . . .

LXX Exo 2.13-15
. . . and (Moses) said to the one doing wrong . . . And he said, Who made thee a ruler and a judge over us? Wouldest thou kill me, as thou killedst the Egyptian yesterday? . . . And Moses departed from the presence of Pharaoh and dwelt in the land of Midian.

MT
. . . and (Moses) said to him that did the wrong, Wherefore smitest thou thy fellow? And he said, Who made thee a prince and a judge over us? thinkest thou to kill me, as thou killedst the Egyptian? . . . But Moses fled from the face of Pharaoh, and dwelt in the land of Midian.

7.32 (cf. Mt 22.32)
I am the God of thy *fathers,*[10] the God of Abraham, and of Isaac, and of Jacob.

Exo 3.6 (cf. 3.15)
I am the God of thy *father,* the God of Abraham, the God of Isaac, and the God of Jacob.

7.35
Who made thee a *ruler* and a judge?

Exo 2.14
Who made thee a *prince* and a judge over us?

7.33-34 (P)
And the Lord said unto him, Loose the shoes from thy feet: for the place whereon thou standest is holy ground. I have surely seen the affliction of my people which is in Egypt, and

Exo 3.5, 7, 8a, 10a
And he said, Draw not nigh hither: put off thy shoes from off thy feet, for the place whereon thou standest is holy ground . . . I have surely seen the affliction of my people which are in

---

[10] "The God of thy fathers": cf. Exo 3.15 "the God of your fathers."

have heard their groaning,[11] and I am come down to deliver them: and now come, I will send thee into Egypt.

Egypt, and have heard their cry . . . and I am come down to deliver them . . . Come now therefore, and I will send thee unto Pharaoh . . .

7.37 (cf. 3.22)
A prophet shall God raise up unto you from among *your* brethren, like unto me.[12]

LXX Deut 18.15
A prophet from among *thy* brethren, like unto me, shall the Lord thy God raise up unto *thee*.

MT
The Lord thy God will raise up unto *thee* a prophet from the midst of thee, of thy brethren, like unto me.

7.40
Make us gods which shall go before us: for as for this Moses, which led us forth out of the land of Egypt, we wot not what is become of him.

Exo 32.1 (cf. 32.23)
Up, make us gods, which shall go before us; for as for this Moses, the man that brought us up out of the land of Egypt, we know not what is become of him.

7.42-43
Did ye offer unto me slain beasts and sacrifices
Forty years in the wilderness, O house of Israel?
And ye took up the tabernacle of Moloch,
And the star of the god Rephan,
The figures which ye made *to worship them*:
And I will carry you away beyond *Babylon*.

LXX Amos 5.25-27
Did ye offer unto me slain beasts and sacrifices
In the wilderness for forty years, O house of Israel?
And ye took up the tabernacle of Moloch,
And the star of your god Raiphan,
Their figures, which you made for *yourselves*;
And I will carry you beyond *Damascus* . . .

MT
Did ye bring unto me sacrifices and *offerings* in the wilderness forty years, O house of Israel?
Yea, ye have borne *Siccuth* your king and *Chium* your images,
The star of your god, which ye made *to yourselves.*
Therefore will I cause you to go into captivity beyond *Damascus* . . .

7.49-50
The heaven is my throne,
And the earth the footstool of my feet:

Isa 66.1-2
The heaven is my throne,
And the earth is my footstool:
What manner of house will ye build unto me?

---

[11] "Groaning": cf. Exo 2.24 "and God heard their groaning."
[12] "Like unto me"; or connecting *hōs eme* with the verb *anastēsei*, "as he raised up me" (ERV fn., RSV).

[33]

What manner of house will ye build me? saith
    the Lord:
Or what is the place of my rest?
Did not my hand make all these things?

And what place shall be my rest?
For all these things hath mine hand made . . .
    saith the Lord.

8.32-33
He was led as a sheep to the slaughter,
He was led as a sheep to the slaughter;
And as a lamb before his shearer is dumb,
So he openeth not his mouth:In his humiliation
    his judgement was taken away:[13]
His generation who shall declare?
For his life is taken from the earth.

LXX Isa 53.7-8
And as a lamb before his shearer is dumb,
So he openeth not his mouth:
In his humiliation his judgment was taken
    away:
His generation who shall declare?

MT
As a lamb that is led to the slaughter,
And as a sheep that before her shearers is
    dumb;
Yea, he opened not his mouth.
By oppression and judgment he was taken away
And as for his generation, who *among them*
    considered that he was cut off out of *the*
    land of the living?

13.18 (A)
And for about forty years suffered he their
manners[14] in the wilderness.

LXX Deut 1.31
And in this wilderness, which ye saw, how the
Lord thy God tenderly bare thee . . .

MT
And in the wilderness, where thou hast seen
how that the Lord thy God bare thee . . .

13.19 (P)
And when he had destroyed seven nations in
the land of Canaan, he gave them their land
for an inheritance . . .

Deut 7.1
When the Lord thy God shall bring thee into
the land whither thou goest to possess it, and
shall cast out many nations before thee . . .
seven nations . . .

13.22 (P)
I have found David the son of Jesse, a man
after my heart, who shall do all my will . . .

Psa 89.20: I have found David . . .
1 Sam 13.14: . . . The Lord hath sought him a
man after his own heart . . .

LXX Isa 44.28: . . . He shall do all my will . . .

---

[13] "His judgement was taken away": or, "justice was denied him" (RSV). The N.T. follows the
LXX literally, which differs considerably from MT "by oppression and judgment he was taken
away."

[14] "Suffered he their manners": translating etropophorēsen, the reading adopted by the majority
of Greek texts. The variant etrophophorēsen "he tenderly bore," adopted by Tischendorf and
Ropes, and preferred by ASV, is the authentic reading in LXX Deut 1.31, translating Heb. nāśā'
"to carry," "to bear."

13.33 (cf. Mt 3.17; Heb 1.5; 5.5)
Thou art my Son,
This day have I begotten thee.

Psa 2.7
Thou art my son;
This day have I begotten thee.

13.34
I will give you the holy and sure blessings[15] of David.

LXX Isa 55.3
... and I will make an everlasting covenant with you, the holy things of David, the sure things.[16]

MT
... and I will make an everlasting covenant with you, even *the sure mercies* of David.

13.35 (cf. 2.27)
Thou wilt not give thy Holy One to see corruption.

LXX Psa 15.10
Neither wilt thou give thy Holy One to see corruption.

MT Psa 16.10
Neither wilt thou *suffer* thine holy one to see corruption.

13.36 (P)
For David . . . fell on sleep, and was laid unto his fathers . . .

1 Kgs 2.10
And David slept with his fathers . . .

13.41
Behold, ye despisers, and wonder, and perish;
For I work a work in your days,
A work which ye shall in no wise believe, if one declare it unto you.

LXX Hab 1.5
Behold, ye despisers, and look, and wonder exceedingly, and perish;[17]
For I work a work in your days,
Which ye shall in no wise believe, if one declare it.

MT
Behold ye among the nations, and regard, and wonder marvelously:
For I work a work in your days,
Which ye will not believe *though* it be told you.

---

[15] There is no word in Greek for "blessings": the phrase ta hosia ta pista means literally "the holy (and) the sure things."

[16] The LXX ta hosia Dauid ta pista is followed literally by the N.T. The MT reads ḥasdey Dawid hane'emānīm "the sure mercies of David" (ERV, ASV, JPS). The LXX apparently took the MT ḥasdey to be ḥasid "godly," "pious," instead of the plural of ḥesed "mercy."

[17] "And wonder exceedingly and perish": the MT reads w^ehitamm^ehu t^emāhu "wonder exceedingly"; there is no explanation for the introduction into the LXX of kai aphanisthēte "and perish."

13.47

I have set thee for a light of the Gentiles,
That thou shouldest be for salvation unto the
    uttermost part of the earth.

LXX Isa 49.6

Behold I have set thee for a covenant of the
    nation, for a light of the Gentiles,
That thou shouldest be for salvation unto the
    uttermost part of the earth.

MT

I will also give thee for a light to the Gentiles,
That thou mayest be my salvation unto the end
    of the earth.

14.15 (A) (cf. 4.24)

. . . God, who made the heaven and the earth
and the sea, and all that in them is.

Exo 20.11 (cf. Psa 146.6)

. . . The Lord made heaven and earth, the sea,
and all that in them is . . .

15.16-18

After these things I will return,
And I will *build again* the tabernacle of David
    which is fallen;
And I will build again the ruins thereof,
And I will set it up:
That the residue of men may seek after the
    Lord,
And all the Gentiles, upon whom my name is
    called,
Saith the Lord, who maketh these things
    known[19] from the beginning of the
    world.[20]

LXX Amos 9.11-12

In that day I will *raise up* the tabernacle of
    David which is fallen;
And I will build again its fallen parts,
And I will raise up the ruins thereof,
And I will built it again as it was in the days of
    old:
That the residue of men and all the Gentiles,
    upon whom my name is called, may seek
    after (me),[18]
Saith the Lord God, who doeth these things.

MT

In that day will I raise up the tabernacle of
    David that is fallen;
And *close up the breaches* thereof;
And I will raise up his ruins, and I will build it
    as in the days of old;
That they may possess the remnant of Edom,
    and all the nations, which are called by
    the name,
Saith the Lord that doeth this.

17.31 (A)

. . . he will judge the world in righteous-
    ness . . .

Psa 9.8 (cf. 96.13; 98.9)

And he shall judge the world in righteous-
    ness . . .

---

[18] "Seek after me": there is no direct object "me" in the LXX, but it is implied by the context.
[19] "Who maketh these things known": the Greek poiōn tauta gnōsta is translated in some versions by "who doeth these things, (which are) known . . ." (cf. the New Dutch Version, Zwingli).
[20] "Who maketh these things known from the beginning of the world": cf. Isa 45.21 "Who hath declared it of old? have not I the Lord?"

23.5
Thou shalt not speak evil of a ruler of thy
    people.

Exo 22.28
Thou shalt not revile God, nor curse a ruler of
    thy people.

28.26-27 (cf. Mt 13.14-15)
Go thou unto this people, and say,
By hearing ye shall hear, and shall in no wise
    understand;
And seeing ye shall see, and shall in no wise
    perceive:
For this people's heart is waxed gross,
And their ears are dull of hearing,
And their eyes they have closed;
Lest haply they should perceive with their
    eyes,
And hear with their ears,
And understand with their heart,
And should turn again,
And I should heal them.

LXX Isa 6.9-10
Go thou and say unto this people,
By hearing ye shall hear, and shall in no wise
    understand;
And seeing ye shall see, and shall in no wise
    perceive:
For this people's heart is waxed gross,
And their ears are dull of hearing,
And their eyes they have closed;
Lest haply they should perceive with their
    eyes,
And hear with their ears,
And understand with their heart,
And should turn again,
And I should heal them.

MT
Go, and tell this people,
Hear ye indeed, but understand not;
And see ye indeed, but perceive not.
Make the heart of this people fat,
And make their ears heavy,
And shut their eyes;
Lest they see with their eyes,
And hear with their ears,
And understand with their heart,
And turn again,
And be healed.[21]

28.28 (A)
. . . This salvation of God is sent unto the
    Gentiles . . .

LXX Psa 66.3
So as to know thy way in the earth,
Thy salvation among all the Gentiles.

MT (Psa 67.2)
That thy way may be known upon earth,
Thy saving health among all nations.

Romans

Romans

Old Testament

1.17 (Gal 3.11; Heb 10.35)
But the righteous shall live by faith.[1]

LXX Hab 2.4
But the righteous shall live by my faith.[2]

---

[21] Cf. footnote to Mt 13.14-15.
[1] Or, "He who through faith is righteous shall live" (RSV; cf. commentaries).

MT
But the just shall live by his faith.

2.6 (A) (cf. Mt 16.27; 2 Tim 4.14)
Who will render to every man according to his works.

LXX Psa 61.13 (cf. Prov 24.12)
For thou renderest to every man according to his works.

MT Psa 62.12
For thou renderest to every man according to his work.

2.24
For the name of God is blasphemed among the Gentiles because of you.

LXX Isa 52.5
Because of you my name is continually blasphemed among the Gentiles.

MT
And my name continually all the day is blasphemed.

3.4
That thou mightest be justified in thy words,
And mightest prevail when thou comest into
    judgment.[3]

LXX Psa 50.6
That thou mightest be justified in thy words,
And mightest prevail when thou comest into
    judgment.

MT Psa 51.4
That thou mayest be justified when thou
    speakest,
And be clear when thou judgest.

3.10-18

There is none righteous,[4] no, not one;

There is none that understandeth,
There is none that seeketh after God;

They have all turned aside, they are together
    become unprofitable;
There is none that doeth good, no, not so much
    as one:

LXX a catena of passages from Psalms
and Isaiah
Psa 13.1: There is none that doeth good, no,
    not so much as one.
Psa 13.2: The Lord looked down from heaven
    ... to see if there is one that under-
    standeth, or one that seeketh after God.
Psa 13.3: They have all turned aside, they are
    together become unprofitable;
There is none that doeth good, no, not so much
    as one.

----

[2] "Faith": or "faithfulness"; the Greek pistis translates the Heb. ʾĕmūnā(h) (cf. Koehler).

[3] "When thou comest into judgment": i.e., "When thou art judged" (cf. RSV).

[4] "There is none righteous": cf. Eccl 7.20 "Surely there is not a righteous man upon earth . . . ."

3.13-18[5]

Their throat is an open sepulchre:	Psa 5.10: Their throat is an open sepulchre,
With their tongues they have used deceit.	With their tongues they have used deceit.
The poison of asps is under their lips:	Psa 139.4: The poison of asps is under their lips.
Whose mouth is full of cursing and bitterness:	Psa 9.28: Whose[6] mouth is full of cursing and bitterness and guile.
Their feet *are swift* to shed blood;	Isa 59.7-8: Their feet in wickedness *run swiftly*
Destruction and misery are in their ways;	to shed blood . . . destruction and misery are
And the way of peace have they not known:	in their ways, and they know not the way of
	peace.
There is no fear of God before *their* eyes.	Psa 35.2: There is no fear of God before *his* eyes.

MT

Psa 14.1: There is none that doeth good.
Psa 14.2: The Lord looked down from heaven upon the children of men, to see if there were any that did understand, that did seek after God.
Psa 14.3: They are all gone aside; they are together become filthy;
There is none that doeth good, no, not one.
Psa 5.9: Their throat is an open sepulchre;
They *flatter* with their tongue
Psa 140.3: Adders' poison is under their lips.
Psa 10.7: *His* mouth is full of cursing *and deceit* and oppression.
Isa 59.7-8: Their feet run to evil, and they make haste to shed innocent blood . . . desolation and destruction are in their paths.
The way of peace they know not.
Psa 36.1: There is no fear of God before *his* eyes.

3.20 (A)	Psa 143.2
Because . . . no flesh shall be justified in his sight.	For in thy sight shall no man living be justified.

4.3 (cf. Jas 2.23a)	LXX Gen 15.6
And Abraham believed God, and it was reckoned unto him for righteousness.	And Abraham believed God, and it was reckoned unto him for righteousness.

---

[5] The words of Rom 3.13-18 are found ipsis litteris in mss. B and Aleph (and others) of LXX Psa 13.3, but not in A and the mass of later mss. It is agreed that these verses formed no part of the original LXX version of Psalm 13 (they are lacking in MT), but were probably interpolated into copies of the LXX from Romans by Christian scribes. From these copies of the LXX they passed over into the Vulgate and its translations, including the Prayer Book of the Church of England (cf. Swete Introduction to the Old Testament in Greek, 251-2).

[6] "Whose": LXX hou, its antecedent being singular "he"; in N.T. hōn, the antecedent is plural "they."

[39]

MT
And he believed *in the Lord*; and *he counted it to him* for righteousness.

4.7-8
Blessed are they whose iniquities are forgiven,
And whose sins are covered.
Blessed is the man to whom the Lord will not
    reckon sin.

LXX Psa 31.1-2a
Blessed are they whose iniquities are forgiven,
And whose sins are covered.
Blessed is the man to whom the Lord will not
    reckon sin.

MT Psa 32.1-2a
Blessed is *he* whose *transgression* is forgiven,
Whose *sin* is covered.
Blessed is the man unto whom the Lord im-
    puteth not iniquity.

4.9 (cf. 4.3)
To Abraham *his faith* was reckoned for righteousness.

LXX Gen 15.6
And Abraham *believed God*, and it was reckoned <u>unto him</u> for righteousness.

MT
And he believed *in the Lord*; and *he counted it to him* for righteousness.

4.17
A father of many nations have I made thee.

LXX Gen 17.5
A father of many nations have I made thee.

MT
The father of *a multitude* of nations have I
made thee.

4.18a
. . . a father of many nations

LXX Gen 17.5
A father of many nations . . . .

4.18
So shall thy seed be.

Gen 15.5
So shall thy seed be.

4.22 (A) (cf. 4.3)
. . . it was reckoned unto him for righteousness

LXX Gen 15.6
And Abraham believed God, and it was reckoned unto him for righteousness.

MT
And he believed in the Lord; and he counted it
to him for righteousness.

7.7 (13.9)
Thou shalt not covet.

Exo 20.17 (Deut 5.21)
Thou shalt not covet.

8.36
For thy sake we are killed all the day long
We *were* accounted as sheep for the slaughter.

Psa 44.22
Yea, for thy sake are we killed all the day
    long;
We *are* counted as sheep for the slaughter.

9.7
In Isaac shall thy seed be called.

Gen 21.12
. . . for in Isaac shall thy seed be called.

9.9
According to this season will I come, and
Sarah shall have a son.

Gen 18.10
I will certainly return unto thee when the
season cometh around;[7] and, lo, Sarah thy wife
shall have a son.

9.12
The elder shall serve the younger.

Gen 25.23
. . . and the elder shall serve the younger.

9.13
Jacob I loved, but Esau I hated.

Mal 1.2-3
. . . yet I loved Jacob, but Esau I hated . . .

9.15
I will have mercy on whom I have mercy, and I
will have compassion on whom I have compassion.

LXX Exo 33.19
I will have mercy on whom I have mercy, and I
will have compassion on whom I have compassion.

MT
And I will be *gracious* to whom I will be *gracious*, and will *shew mercy* on whom I will
shew mercy.

9.17
For this very purpose *did I raise thee up*, that I
might shew in thee my *power*, and that my
name might be published abroad in all the
earth.

LXX Exo 9.16
For this very purpose *you were preserved*, that
I might shew in thee my *strength*,[8] and that
my name might be published abroad in all the
earth.

---

7 "When the season cometh around": RSV "in the spring."

[41]

MT
But in very deed for this cause have I made thee to stand, for *to shew* thee my power, and that my name may be declared throughout all the earth.

9.20 (A)
Shall the thing formed say to him that formed it, Why didst thou make me thus?

Isa 29.16 (cf. 45.9)
Shall the potter be counted as clay; that the thing made should say of him that made it, He made me not . . .

9.21 (A)
Or hath not the potter a right over the
    clay . . . ?

Jer 18.6
Behold, as the clay in the potter's hand, so are ye in mine hand . . .

9.25 (cf. 1 Peter 2.10)
I will call that my people, which was not my
    people,
And her beloved, which was not beloved.

Hos 2.23
. . . and I will have mercy upon her that had not obtained mercy; and I will say to them which were not my people, Thou art my people . . .

9.26
And it shall be, that in the place where it was
    said unto them, Ye are not my people,
There shall they be called sons of the living
    God.

LXX Hos 2.1
And it shall be, that in the place where it was
    said unto them, Ye are not my people,
There shall they be called sons of the living
    God.

MT (Hos 1.10)
And it shall come to pass that, in the place
    where it was said unto them, Ye are not
    my people,
It shall be said unto them, *Ye are the sons of*
    the living God.

9.27-28
If the number of *the children* of Israel be as the sand of the sea, it is *the* remnant that shall be saved: for *the Lord* will execute his word upon the earth, finishing it and cutting it short.

LXX Isa 10.22-23 (cf. Hos 1.10a)
And if *the people* of Israel become as the sand of the sea, it is *their* remnant that shall be saved: for *God* will execute his word in righteousness upon the whole earth, finishing it and cutting it short . . .

MT
For though thy people Israel be as the sand of the sea, only a remnant of them shall return . . . *For a consummation, and that determined,*

---

[8] "Strength": LXX *ischun*; N.T. *dunamin* "power."

shall the Lord, the Lord of hosts, make in the
midst of all the earth.

9.29
Except the Lord of Sabaoth had left us a seed,
We had become as Sodom, and had been made
like unto Gomorrah.

LXX Isa 1.9
Except the Lord of Sabaoth had left us a seed,
We had become as Sodom, and had been made
like unto Gomorrah.

MT
Except the Lord of hosts had left unto us a
very small remnant, we should have been as
Sodom, we should have been like unto Gomorrah.

9.33 (P) (10.11; 1 Peter 2.6, 8)
Behold, I lay in Zion a stone of stumbling and a
rock *of offence:*
And he that believeth on him shall not be put
to shame.

LXX Isa 28.16 and MT Isa 8.14
Behold, I place in the foundations of Zion a
stone . . . and he that believeth on him shall
not be put to shame. . . . But for a stone of
stumbling and for a rock of offence.

MT Isa 28.16
Behold I lay in Zion for a foundation a stone
. . . he that believeth *shall not make haste.*

10.5 (P) (Gal 3.12)
. . . the man that doeth the righteousness
which is of the law shall live thereby.

Lev 18.5
Ye shall therefore keep my statutes, and my
judgments: which if a man do, he shall live in
them . . .

10.6-8 (P)
. . . Say not in thy heart, Who shall ascend into
heaven? . . . or, Who shall descend into the
abyss? . . . The word is nigh thee, in thy
mouth, and in thy heart . . .

Deut 9.4 and 30.12-14
Speak not thou in thine heart . . .
Who shall go up for us to heaven . . . ? Who
shall go over the sea for us . . . ? But the
word is very nigh unto thee, in thy mouth, and
in thy heart . . .

10.11 (cf. 9.33)
Whosoever believeth on him shall not be put to
shame.

LXX Isa 28.16
. . . and he that believeth on him shall not be
put to shame.

MT
. . . he that believeth *shall not make haste.*

10.13 (cf. Acts 2.21)
Whosoever shall call upon the name of the
Lord shall be saved.

LXX Joel 3.5[9]
Whosoever shall call upon the name of the
Lord shall be saved.

MT
Whosoever shall call on the name of the Lord shall be *delivered*.

10.15 (Eph 6.15)
How beautiful are the feet of *them* that bring glad tidings of good things!

Isa 52.7 (cf. Nahum 1.15)
How beautiful upon the mountains are the feet of *him* that bringeth good tidings . . . that bringeth good tidings of good . . .

10.16 (cf. Jn 12.38)
Lord, who hath believed our report?

LXX Isa 53.1
Lord, who hath believed our report?

MT
Who hath believed our report?

10.18
Their sound went out into all the earth,
And their words unto the ends of the world.

LXX Psa 18.5
Their sound went out into all the earth,
And their words unto the ends of the world.

MT Psa 19.4
Their *line* is gone out through all the earth,
And their words to the end of the world.

10.19
I will provoke *you* to jealousy with that which
  is no nation,
With a nation void of understanding will I
  anger *you.*

LXX Deut 32.21
I will provoke *them* to jealousy with that
  which is no nation,
With a nation void of understanding will I
  anger *them.*

MT
And I will move *them* to jealousy with *those*
  which are not *a people.*
I will provoke *them* to anger with a foolish
  nation.

10.20
I was found of them that sought me not;
I became manifest unto them that asked not of
  me.

LXX Isa 65.1
I became manifest unto them that sought me
  not,
I was found by them that asked not of me.

MT
I am *inquired of* by them that asked not for
  me;
I am found of them that sought me not.

---

9 Joel 3.5 in LXX and MT; in English Versions, 2.32.

10.21
All the day long did I spread out my hands unto
a disobedient and gainsaying people.

LXX Isa 65.2
I spread out my hands all the day long unto a
disobedient and gainsaying people.

MT
I have spread out my hands all the day unto a
*rebellious people, which walketh in a way that
is not good, after their own thoughts.*

11.2 (A)
God did not cast off his people . . .

Psa 94.14 (cf. 1 Sam 12.22)
For the Lord will not cast off his people.

11.3
Lord, they have killed thy prophets, they have
digged down thine altars: and I am left alone,
and they seek my life.

1 Kgs 19.10 (19.14)
For *the children of Israel* have . . . thrown
down thine altars, and slain thy prophets with
the sword: and I, even I only, am left; and they
seek my life . . .

11.4
I have left for myself seven thousand men,
who have not bowed the knee to Baal.

1 Kgs 19.18
Yet *will I leave* me seven thousand in Israel,
all the knees which have not bowed unto
Baal . . .

11.8
God gave them a spirit of stupor,
Eyes that they should not see, and ears that
     they should not hear, unto this very day.

Isa 29.10 and Deut 29.4
For the Lord hath poured out upon you the
     spirit of deep sleep . . .
But the Lord hath not given you an heart to
     know, and the eyes to see, and ears to
hear, unto this day.

11.9-10
Let their table be made a snare, and a trap,
And a stumblingblock, and a recompense unto
     them:
Let their eyes be darkened, that they may not
     see,
And bow thou down their back alway.

LXX Psa 68.23-24
Let their table before them be made a snare,
And a recompense and a stumblingblock:
Let their eyes be darkened, that they may not
     see,
And bow thou down their back alway.

MT Psa 69.22-23
Let their table before them become a snare;
And when they are in peace, let it become a
     trap.
Let their eyes be darkened, that they see not;
And *make their loins continually to shake.*

Romans

11.26-27

There shall come *out of* Zion the Deliverer;
He shall turn away ungodliness from Jacob:
And this is my covenant unto them,
When I shall take away *their sins.*

LXX Isa 59.20-21 and 27.9 (cf. Jer
31.33-34
And the Deliverer shall come *on account of*
    Zion,
And he shall turn away ungodliness from
    Jacob.
. . . When I shall take away *his sin* . . .

MT
And a redeemer shall come *to* Zion, *and unto
them that turn from the transgression in*
Jacob, saith the Lord. And as for me, this is
my covenant with them . . .
. . . and this is all the fruit of taking away *his
sin* . . .

11.34 (1 Cor 2.16)
For who hath known the mind of the Lord?
Or who hath been his counsellor?

LXX Isa 40.13
Who hath known the mind of the Lord?
And who hath been his counsellor . . . ?

MT
Who hath *directed the spirit* of the Lord,
Or being his counsellor hath taught him?

11.35
Or who hath first given to *him,* and *it shall be
recompensed* unto him again?

Job 41.11
Who hath first given unto *me,* that *I should
repay* him?

12.17 (P) (cf. 2 Cor 8.21)
Take thought for things honorable in the sight
of all men.

LXX Prov 3.4
Take thought for things honorable in the sight
of the Lord and of men.

MT
So shalt thou find favour and good understanding in the sight of God and man.

12.19 (Heb 10.30)
Vengeance belongeth unto me: I will recompense . . .

Deut 32.35
MT: Vengeance is mine, and recompense . . .

LXX: In the day of vengeance I will recompense . . .

12.20
But if thine enemy hunger, feed him; if he
thirst, give him to drink: for in so doing thou
heap coals of fire upon his head.

LXX Prov 25.21-22
If thine enemy hunger, feed him; if he thirst,
give him to drink: for in so doing thou shalt
shalt heap coals of fire upon his head.

MT
If thine enemy be hungry, *give him bread* to
    eat;
And if he be thirsty, *give him water* to drink:
For thou shalt heap coals of fire upon his
    head . . .

13.9a (cf. Mt 19.18)
Thou shalt not commit adultery, Thou shalt
not kill,[10] Thou shalt not steal, Thou shalt not
covet.

Exo 20.13-15, 17 (Deut 5.17-19, 21)
Thou shalt do no murder. Thou shalt not
commit adultery. Thou shalt not steal. Thou
shalt not covet . . .

13.9b (cf. Mt 19.19)
Thou shalt love thy neighbour as thyself.

Lev 19.18
. . . thou shalt love thy neighbour as thyself.

14.11
As I live, saith the Lord, to me every knee
    shall bow,
And every tongue shall confess to God.

Isa 49.18 and LXX 45.23
As I live, saith the Lord . . .
. . . For to me every knee shall bow,
And every tongue shall confess to God.

MT
As I live, saith the Lord . . .
. . . Unto me every knee shall bow, every
    tongue shall *swear.*

15.3
The reproaches of them that reproached thee
    fell upon me.

LXX Psa 68.10
The reproaches of them that reproached thee
fell upon me.

MT Psa 69.9
The reproaches of them that *reproach* thee are
fallen upon me.

15.9
Therefore will I give *praise* unto thee among
    the Gentiles,
And sing unto thy name.

Psa 18.49 (2 Sam 22.50)
Therefore I will give *thanks* unto thee, <u>O Lord</u>,
    among the nations,
And will sing praises unto thy name.

15.10
Rejoice, ye Gentiles, with his people.

LXX Deut 32.43
Rejoice, ye Gentiles, with his people.
MT
Rejoice, O ye nations, with his people.

---

[10] "Kill": The Greek <u>phoneuō</u> may also mean "to murder."

[47]

Romans

15.11
Praise the Lord, all ye Gentiles;
And *let* all the peoples *praise* him.

Psa 117.1
O praise the Lord, all ye nations;
Laud him, all *ye* peoples.

15.12
There shall be the root of Jesse,
And he that ariseth to rule over the Gentiles;
On him shall the Gentiles hope.

LXX Isa 11.10
And there shall be in that day the root of
    Jesse,
And he that ariseth to rule over the Gentiles;
On him shall the Gentiles hope.
MT
And it shall come to pass in that day, that the
root of Jesse, which standeth for an ensign of
the peoples, unto him shall the nations seek;
and his resting place shall be glorious.

15.21
They shall see, to whom no tidings of him
    came,
And they who have not heart shall understand.

LXX Isa 52.15
For they shall see, to whom no tidings of him
    came,
And they who have not heard shall understand.

MT
For *that which had not been told them* shall
    thy see;
And *that which they had not heard* shall they
    understand.

1 Corinthians

1 Corinthians

Old Testament

1.19
I will destroy the wisdom of the wise,
And the prudence of the prudent *will I reject.*

LXX Isa 29.14
I will destroy the wisdom of the wise,
And the prudence of the prudent *I will hide.*

MT
And the wisdom of *their* wise men *shall perish,*
And the understanding of *their* prudent men
    shall be hid.

1.31 (2 Cor 10.17)
He that glorieth, let him glory in the Lord.

Jer 9.24
But let him that glorieth glory in this, that he
understandeth and knoweth me, that I am the
Lord . . .

2.9
Things which eye saw not, and ear heard not,
And which entered not into the heart of man,[1]

Isa 64.4 (cf. 52.15)
For from of old men have not heard, nor
perceived by the ear, neither hath the eye

Whatsoever things God *prepared for them that love him.*

seen a God beside thee, *which worketh for him that waiteth for him.*

2.16 (cf. Rom 11.34)
For who hath known the mind of the Lord, that he should instruct him?

LXX Isa 40.13
Who hath known the mind of the Lord. And who hath been his counsellor, who instructeth him?

MT
Who hath *directed the spirit* of the Lord, or being his counsellor hath taught him?

3.19
He that taketh the wise in their craftiness.

Job 5.13
He taketh the wise in their own craftiness . . .

3.20
The Lord knoweth the reasonings of *the wise,* that they are vain.

LXX Psa 93.11
The Lord knoweth the reasoning of *men,* that they are vain.

MT Psa 94.11
The Lord knoweth the *thoughts* of *man,* that they are vanity.

5.13 (P)
Put away the wicked man from among yourselves.

LXX Deut 17.7 (19.19; 22.24; 24.7)
And thou[2] shalt put away the wicked man from among yourselves.

MT
So thou shalt put away *the evil* from the midst of thee.

6.16 (cf. Mt 19.5)
The twain . . . shall become one flesh.

LXX Gen 2.24
. . . and the twain shall become one flesh.

MT
. . . and *they* shall be one flesh.

9.9 (1 Tim 5.18)
Thou shalt not muzzle the ox when he treadeth out the corn.

Deut 25.4
Thou shalt not muzzle the ox when he treadeth out the corn.

----

[1] "Which entered not into the heart of man": cf. LXX Jer 3.16 "it shall not enter the heart."
[2] "You" in LXX is sg.: in N.T. the verb is plural.

[49]

1 Corinthians

10.5 (A)	LXX Num 14.16
... for they were overthrown in the wilderness.	The Lord ... overthrew them in the wilderness.
	MT
	... (The Lord) hath slain them in the wilderness.

| 10.7 | Exo 32.6 |
| The people sat down to eat and drink, and rose up to play. | ... and the people sat down to eat and to drink, and rose up to play. |

10.20 (A)	LXX Deut 32.17
... they sacrifice to demons, and not to God ...	They sacrificed to demons, and not to God.
	MT
	They sacrificed unto demons, which were no God.

| 10.22 (A) | Deut 32.21 |
| Or do we provoke the Lord to jealousy? | They have moved me to jealousy with that which is not God. |

| 10.26 | Psa 24.1 |
| For the earth is the Lord's, and the fullness thereof. | The earth is the Lord's, and the fullness thereof. |

| 14.21 | Isa 28.11-12 |
| By men of strange tongues and by the lips of strangers *will I speak* unto this people; and not even thus will they hear me ... | Nay, but by men of strange lips and with another tongue *will he speak* to this people ... yet they would not hear. |

| 15.25 (A) (cf. Mt 22.44) | Psa 110.1 |
| ... till he hath put all his enemies under his feet. | ... Sit thou at my right hand, until I make thine enemies thy footstool. |

| 15.27 (P) | Psa 8.6 |
| He put all things in subjection under his feet. | ... Thou hast put all things under his feet. |

| 15.32 | Isa 22.13 |
| ... let us eat and drink, for tomorrow we die. | ... let us eat and drink, for tomorrow we shall die. |

15.45 (P) The first man Adam became a living soul.	Gen 2.7 ... and man[3] became a living soul.

15.47 (A) The first man is of the earth, earthy ...	Gen 2.7 And the Lord God formed man of the dust of the ground ...

15.54 Death is swallowed up[4] *in victory.*[5]	Isa 25.8 MT: He hath swallowed up death *for ever.* Theodotion: Death is swallowed up in victory.

15.55 O death, where is thy *victory?* O *death,* where is thy sting?	LXX Hos 13.14 Where is thy *punishment,* O death? Where is thy sting, O *Hades?* MT O death, where are thy *plagues?* O *grave,* where is thy *destruction?*

2 Corinthians

2 Corinthians	Old Testament
3.7 (A) ... Moses ... the glory of his face ...	Exo 34.35 ... the skin of Moses' face shone ...

3.13 (A) ... Moses ... put a veil upon his face ...	Exo 34.35 (34.33) ... Moses put the veil upon his face ...

3.16 (A) But whensoever it[1] shall turn to the Lord, the veil is taken away.	Exo 34.34 But when Moses went in before the Lord ... he took the veil off. ...

---

[3] "Man": in Heb. 'ādām.

[4] "Is swallowed up": the MT has the active form of the verb, billa', "he hath swallowed up"; the N.T. passive form represents the Heb. bulla'. The Greek O.T. translations of Theodotion and Symmachus, like Paul, have the passive form of the verb katopothē (cf. Kittle's note to Isa 25.8).

[5] "In victory": the MT reads lānesah "forever," a phrase which the LXX translates eis nikos in several passages (cf. 2 Sam 2.26; Job 36.7; Jer 3.5; Lam 3.18; 5.20; Amos 1.11; 8.7). In Isa 25.8, however, which Paul is quoting, LXX has ischusas "being strong"; Theodotion, like Paul, has eis nikos.

[1] "It": or, impersonally, "a man" (ERV fn., RSV).

4.13
I believed, and therefore did I speak.

LXX Psa 115.1
I believed, and therefore did I speak.

MT Psa 116.10
I believe, *for I will* speak.

6.2
At an acceptable time I hearkened unto thee,
And in a day of salvation did I succour thee.

LXX Isa 49.8
At an acceptable time I hearkened unto thee,
And in a day of salvation did I succour
    thee . . .

MT
In an acceptable time have I *answered* thee,
And in a day of salvation have I *helped*
    thee . . .

6.16 (P)
I will dwell in them, and walk in them;
And I will be their God, and they shall be my
    people.

Lev 26.12 and Ezek 37.27
And I will walk among you, and will be your
    God, and ye shall be my people.
My tabernacle also shall be with them; and I
    will be their God, and they shall be my
    people.

6.17 (P)
Come ye out from among them, and be ye
    separate, saith the Lord,
And touch no unclean thing;
And I will receive you.

LXX Isa 52.11 (cf. Jer 51.45)
. . . Come ye out thence and touch no unclean
    thing; come out from her midst, be ye
    separate . . .

MT
Depart ye, depart ye, go ye out from thence,
    touch no unclean thing; go ye out of the
    midst of her; be ye clean . . .

LXX Ezek 20.34 (cf. 20.41)
And I will receive you from the countries . . .

MT
And I will bring you out from the peoples . . .

6.18 (P)
And I will be to you a Father,
These things saith the Lord Almighty . . .
and ye shall be to me sons and daughters, saith
    the Lord Almighty.

LXX 2 Sam 7.8, 14 (cf. Isa 43.6)
. . . I shall be to him a father, and he shall be
    to me a son.

MT
Thus saith the Lord of hosts . . .
. . . I will be his father, and he shall be my *son.*

8.15
He that gathered much had nothing over; and
   he that gathered little had no lack.

Exo 16.18
... He that gathered much had nothing over,
   and he that gathered little had no
   lack ...

8.21 (P) (cf. Rom 12.17)
For we take thought for things honourable, not
   only in the sight of the Lord, but also in
   the sight of men.

LXX Prov 3.4
Take thought for things honourable in the sight
   of the Lord and of men.

MT
So shalt thou find favour and good understanding in the sight of God and man.

9.7 (A)
... For God loveth a cheerful giver.

LXX Prov 22.8
God blesses the cheerful and generous man.

MT
No equivalent to the LXX passage.

9.9
He hath scattered abroad, he hath given to the
   poor;
His righteousness abideth for ever.

Psa 112.9
He hath dispersed, he hath given to the needy;
His righteousness endureth for ever ...

10.17 (cf. 1 Cor 1.31)
But he that glorieth, let him glory in the Lord.

Jer 9.24
But let him that glorieth glory in this, that he
   understandeth and knoweth me, that I am
   the Lord ...

13.1 (A) (cf. MT 18.16)
At the mouth of two witnesses or three shall
every word[2] be established.

LXX Deut 19.15
... At the mouth of two witnesses and at the
mouth of three witnesses every word[2] shall be
established ...

MT
... At the mouth of two witnesses, or at the
   mouth of three witnesses, shall a
   matter[2] be established.

---

[2] "Word" or "matter": Gk. rēma; Heb. dābār.

Galatians

Galatians	Old Testament
1.15 (A) ... God ... separated me, from my mother's womb, and called me ...	LXX Isa 49.1 (cf. Jer 1.5) ... from my mother's womb he called my name ... MT ... the Lord hath called me from the womb ...
2.16 (A) (cf. Rom 3.20) ... shall no flesh be justified.	Psa 143.2 For in thy sight shall no man living be justified.
3.6 (cf. Rom 4.3) ... Abraham believed God, and it was reckoned unto him for righteousness.	LXX Gen 15.6 And Abraham believed God, and it was reckoned unto him for righteousness. MT And he believed *in the Lord*; and *he counted it to him* for righteousness.
3.8 (cf. Acts 3.25) In thee shall all the *nations* be blessed.	Gen 12.3 (cf. 18.18) ... and in thee shall all the *families of the earth* be blessed.[1]
3.10 Cursed is every one which continueth not in all *the things that are written in the book of the law*, to do them.	LXX Deut 27.26 Cursed is every man which continueth not all *the words of this law*, to do them. MT Cursed be he that *confirmeth* not *the words of this law* to do them.
3.11 (cf. Rom 1.17) The righteous shall live by faith.[2]	LXX Hab 2.4 But the righteous shall live by <u>my</u> faith.[3]

---

[1] "Shall be blessed": or "shall bless themselves" (RSV).

[2] Or, "He who through faith is righteous shall live" (RSV; cf. commentaries).

MT
But the just shall live by his faith.

3.12 (cf. Rom 10.5)
He that doeth them shall live in them.

Lev 18.5
. . . which, if a man do, he shall live in
them . . .

3.13
Cursed is every one that hangeth on a tree.

LXX Deut 21.23
. . . for accursed of God is every one that
hangeth on a tree.

MT
. . . for he that is hanged is accursed of God.

3.16
And to thy seed.

Gen 13.15 (12.7; 17.7, 8; 24.7)
. . . and to thy seed . . .

4.27
Rejoice, thou barren that bearest not;
Break forth and cry, thou that travailest not:
For more are the children of the desolate,
Than of her which hath the husband.

LXX Isa 54.1
Rejoice, thou barren that bearest not;
Break forth and cry, thou that travailest not:
For more are the children of the desolate,
Than of her which hath the husband.

MT
Sing, O barren, thou that didst not bear;
Break forth *into singing*, and cry aloud, thou
        that didst not travail with child:
For more are the children of the desolate
Than the children of the married wife . . .

4.30
Cast out the handmaid and her son: for the son
of the handmaid shall not inherit with the son
of the freewoman.

Gen 21.10
Cast out this bondwoman and her son: for the
son of this bondwoman shall not be heir with
my son, even with Isaac.

5.14 (cf. Mt 19.19)
Thou shalt love thy neighbour as thyself.

Lev 19.18
Thou shalt love thy neighbour as thyself.

---

3 "Faith": or "faithfulness"; the Gk. pistis translates the Heb. ʾĕmūnā(h) (cf. Koehler).

[55]

Ephesians

<table>
<tr><td>Ephesians</td><td>Old Testament</td></tr>
<tr><td>

1.20 (A) (cf. Mt 22.44)
... and made him to sit at his right hand ...
</td><td>

Psa 110.1
... Sit thou at my right hand ...
</td></tr>
<tr><td>

1.22 (A) (cf. 1 Cor 15.27)
... and he put all things in subjection under his feet ...
</td><td>

Psa 8.6
... Thou hast put all things under his feet.
</td></tr>
<tr><td>

2.17 (A)
... and he preached peace to you that were far off, and peace to them that were nigh.
</td><td>

LXX Isa 57.19 (cf. 52.7)
... peace to those who are far off, and to those who are near ...

MT
... Peace, peace, to him that is far off and to *him* that is near ...
</td></tr>
<tr><td>

4.8
When he ascended on high, he led captivity captive,
And gave gifts *unto* men.
</td><td>

Psa 68.18
Thou hast ascended on high, thou hast led <u>thy</u> captivity captive;
Thou has received gifts *among* men ...
</td></tr>
<tr><td>

4.25 (A)
... Speak ye truth each one with his neighbour ...
</td><td>

Zech 8.16
Speak ye every man the truth with his neighbour ...
</td></tr>
<tr><td>

4.26 (A)
Be ye angry, and sin not ...
</td><td>

LXX Psa 4.4
Be ye angry, and sin not ...

MT Psa 4.5
Stand in awe,[1] and sin not ...
</td></tr>
</table>

---

[1] "Stand in awe": ERV; ERV fn., RSV "Be ye angry." The Heb. <u>rigzū</u> means "tremble" (see JPS).

5.14 Awake, thou that sleepest, and arise from the dead. And Christ shall shine upon thee.	No O.T. passage.[2]
5.18 (A) And be not drunken with wine . . .	LXX Prov 23.31 Be not drunken with wine . . . MT Look not thou upon the wine when it is red . . .

5.31 (cf. Mt 19.5) For this cause shall a man leave his father and mother, and shall cleave to his wife, and the twain shall become one flesh.	LXX Gen 2.24 For this cause shall a man leave his father and *his* mother, and shall cleave to his wife; and the twain shall become one flesh. MT Therefore shall a man leave his father and his mother, and shall cleave unto his wife: and *they* shall be one flesh.

6.2-3 (cf. Mt 15.4) Honour thy father and mother . . . that it may be well with thee, and thou mayest live long *on the earth.*	LXX Deut 5.16 (Exo 20.12) Honour thy father and thy mother, <u>as the Lord thy God commanded thee</u>, that it may be well with thee, and that thou mayest live long *in the land* that the Lord thy God giveth thee. MT Honour thy father and thy mother, <u>as the Lord thy God commanded thee</u>: that thy days may be long, and that it may go well with thee, *upon the land* which the Lord thy God giveth thee.

6.14-15 (A) . . . having girded your loins with truth, and having put on the breastplate of righteousness, and having shod your feet with the preparation of the gospel of peace . . .	LXX Isa 11.5; MT Isa 59.17; 52.7 . . . and he shall have his loin girded with righteousness, and his sides covered with truth . . . . . . and he put on righteousness as a breastplate . . . . . . the feet of him that bringeth good tidings, that publisheth peace . . . MT Isa 11.5 And righteousness shall be the girdle of his loins, and faithfulness the girdle of his reins.

---

[2] It is conjectured that this quotation is taken either from an unknown Christian apocryphal work, or a Christian hymn. It is to be noticed that it is introduced with the same formula which introduces the quotation at 4.8, <u>dio legei</u>: either impersonally "Therefore it is said" (RSV) or, less probably, "Therefore he says" (ERV).

Ephesians

6.17 (A)
... the helmet of salvation ...

Isa 59.17
... a helmet of salvation upon his head ...

6.17 (A)
... the sword of the Spirit, which is the word
of God.

LXX Isa 11.4; MT Isa 49.2; Hos 6.5
... and he shall smite the earth with the word
of his mouth and with the breath through
his lips he shall kill the ungodly
... he hath made my mouth like a sharp
sword ...
... I have slain them by the words of my
mouth ...

MT Isa 11.4
... and he shall smite the earth with the rod
of his mouth, and with the breath of his
lips shall he slay the wicked.

Philippians

Old Testament

1.19 (A)
For I know that this shall turn to my salvation ...

LXX Job 13.16
This shall turn to my salvation ...

MT
This also shall be my salvation ...

2.10-11 (A)
That in the name of Jesus every knee should
bow, of things in heaven and things on earth
and things under the earth, and that every
tongue should confess that Jesus Christ is Lord
...

LXX Isa 45.23
... unto me every knee shall bow, and every
tongue shall confess to God ...

MT
... unto me every knee shall bow, every
tongue shall swear.

Colossians

Colossians

Old Testament

2.22 (A) (cf. Mt 15.9)
... the precepts and doctrines of men.

LXX Isa 29.13
... the precepts of men and doctrines.

MT
... a commandment of men which hath been
taught them.

3.1 (A) (cf. Mt 22.44)
... where Christ is, seated on the right hand of God.

Psa 110.1
... Sit thou at my right hand ...

1 Thessalonians

1 Thessalonians	Old Testament
5.8 (A) (cf. Eph 6.14, 17) ... putting on the breastplate of faith and love; and for a helmet, the hope of salvation.	Isa 59.17 And he put on righteousness as a breastplate, and an helmet of salvation upon his head ...

2 Thessalonians

2 Thessalonians

Old Testament

1.8 (A)
... in flaming fire, rendering vengeance to them that know not God ...

LXX Isa 66.15
... to render vengeance in wrath and damnation in flaming fire ...
Jer 10.25 (cf. Psa 79.6)
Pour out thy fury upon the heathen that know thee not ...

MT Isa 66.15
... to render his anger with fury, and his rebuke with flames of fire.

1.9 (A)
... from the face of the Lord and from the glory of his might ...

LXX Isa 2.20 (2.19, 21)
... from the presence[1] of the fear of the Lord and from the glory of his might ...

MT
... from before the terror of the Lord, and from the glory of his majesty.

2.4 (A)
... he that exalteth himself against all that is called God ...

... he sitteth in the temple of God, setting himself forth as God.

Dan 11.36
... he shall exalt himself ... above every god ...
Ezek 28.2
I sit in the seat of God ... thou didst set thy heart as the heart of God.

---

[1] "Presence": Gk. prosōpon "face."

2 Thessalonians

2.8 (A)	Isa 11.4
. . . the lawless one, whom the Lord Jesus shall slay with the breath of his mouth . . .	. . . and with the breath of his lips shall he slay the wicked.

1 Timothy

1 Timothy   Old Testament

5.18a (cf. 1 Cor 9.9)	Deut 25.4
Thou shalt not muzzle the ox when he treadeth out the corn.	Thou shalt not muzzle the ox when he treadeth out the corn.

----------------   ----------

5.18b	No O.T. passage.[1]
The labourer is worthy of his hire.	

----------------   ----------------

5.19 (A) (cf. Mt 18.16)	LXX Deut 19.15
. . . except at the mouth of two or three witnesses.	. . . At the mouth of two witnesses and at the mouth of three witnesses every word shall be established.
	MT
	. . . At the mouth of two witnesses, or at the mouth of three witnesses, shall a matter be established.

2 Timothy

2 Timothy   Old Testament

2.19 (A)	LXX Num 16.5
The Lord knoweth them that are his.	God looks upon and knows them that are his.
	MT
	. . . the Lord will shew who are his . . .

----------------   ----------------

4.14 (A) (cf. Rom 2.6)	LXX Psa 61.13 (cf. Prov 24.12)
. . . the Lord will render to him according to his works.	For thou renderest to every man according to his works.

---

[1] The manner in which this saying is cited in 1 Timothy 5.18 places it in the same category with the quotation of Deut 25.4 in the first part of the verse. The saying is not found in the O.T., but it appears ipsis litteris in Luke 10.7 as a saying of Jesus.

MT Psa 62.12
For thou renderest to every man according to
his work.

Titus

Titus	Old Testament
2.14 (A) ... that he might redeem us from all iniquity, and purify unto himself a people for his own possession ...	Psa 130.8; Ezek 37.23; Deut 14.2 And he shall redeem Israel from all his iniquities. ... but I ... will cleanse them: so shall they be my people, and I will be their God. ... the Lord hath chosen thee to be a peculiar people unto himself ...

Hebrews

Hebrews	Old Testament
1.3 (A) (cf. Mt 22.44) ... he sat down on the right hand of the Majesty on high.	Psa 110.1 Sit thou at my right hand ...

1.5a (5.5; cf. Acts 13.33) Thou art my Son, This day have I begotten thee.	Psa 2.7 Thou art my son; This day have I begotten thee.

1.5b (cf. 2 Cor 6.18) I will be to him a Father, And he shall be to me a Son.	2 Sam 7.14 I will be his father, And he shall be my son.[1]

1.6 And let all *the angels*[2] of God worship him.	LXX Deut 32.43 And let all *the sons* of God worship him. MT No equivalent to the LXX passage.

1.7 Who maketh his angels winds,	LXX Psa 103.4 Who maketh his angels winds,

---

[1] Literally, "I will be to him for a father, and he shall be to me for a son" (JPS); so also LXX.
[2] "Angels": cf. LXX Psa 96.7: "Worship ye him, all his angels."

[61]

And his ministers *a flame of fire.*

And his ministers *a flaming fire.*

MT Psa 104.4
Who maketh *winds his messengers*;
His ministers a flaming fire.

1.8-9
Thy throne, O God, is for ever and ever;
And the sceptre of uprightness is the sceptre
    of thy kingdom.
Thou hast loved righteousness, and hated
    iniquity;
Therefore God, thy God hath anointed thee
With the oil of gladness above thy fellows.

Psa 45.6-7
Thy throne, O God, is for ever and ever:
A sceptre of equity is the sceptre of thy
    kingdom.
Thou hast loved righteousness, and hated
    wickedness:
Therefore God, thy God hath anointed thee
With the oil of gladness above thy fellows.

1.10-12
Thou, Lord, in the beginning hast laid the
    foundation of the earth,
And the heavens are the works of thy hands:
They shall perish; but thou continuest:
And they all shall wax old as doth a garment;
And as a mantle shalt thou roll them up,
As a garment, and they shall be changed:
But thou art the same,
And thy years shall not fail:

LXX Psa 101.26-28
In the beginning thou, Lord, hast laid the
    foundation of the earth,
And the heavens are the works of thy hands:
They shall perish; but thou continuest:
And they all shall wax old as doth a garment;
And as a mantle shalt thou roll them up,
And they shall be changed.
But thou art the same,
And thy years shall not fail.

MT Psa 102.25-27
Of old hast thou laid the foundation of the
earth;
And the heavens are the work of thy hands.
They shall perish, but thou shalt endure:
Yea, all of them shall wax old like a garment;
As a vesture shalt thou *change* them, and they
    shall be changed:
But thou art the same,
And thy years *shall have no end.*

1.13 (cf. Mt 22.44)
Sit thou on my right hand,
Till I put thine enemies as a footstool of thy
    feet.

LXX Psa 109.1
Sit thou on my right hand,
Till I put thine enemies as a footstool of thy
    feet.

MT Psa 110.1
Sit thou at my right hand,
Until I make thine enemies thy footstool.

2.6-8
What is man, that thou art mindful of him?
Or the son of man, that thou visitest him?
Thou madest him a little lower than *the
    angels*;

Psa 8.4-6
What is man, that thou art mindful of him?
And the son of man, that thou visitest him?
For thou hast made him but little lower than
    God

Thou crownedst him with glory and honour,
And *didst set him over* the works of thy
hands.[4]
Thou didst put all things in <u>subjection</u> under
his feet.

And crownest him with glory and honour.
Thou *madest him to have dominion over* the
works of thy hands;
Thou hast put all things under his feet.

2.12
I will declare thy name unto my brethren,
In the midst of the congregation will I sing thy
praise.

Psa 22.22
I will declare thy name unto my brethren:
In the midst of the congregation will I praise
thee.

2.13a
I will put my trust in him.

LXX Isa 8.17 (cf. 2 Sam 22.3)
. . . I will put my trust in him.

MT
. . . I will *look for* him.

2.13b
Behold, I and the children which God hath
given me.

LXX Isa 8.18
Behold, I and the children which God hath
given me . . .

MT
Behold, I and the children whom *the Lord* hath
given me . . .

2.16 (A)
. . . but he taketh hold of the seed of Abraham.

Isa 41.8-9
. . . the seed of Abraham my friend; thou
whom I have taken hold of from the ends of
the earth . . .

3.2, 5 (A)
. . . who was faithful . . . as also was Moses in
all his house.
And Moses indeed was faithful in all his house
as a servant . . .

Num 12.7
My servant Moses is not so; he is faithful in all
mine house.

3.7-11
Today if ye shall hear his voice,

LXX Psa 94.7-11
Today if ye shall hear his voice,

---

[3] "God": or "gods" or "angels": the Hebrew ʾelohim may mean any one of the three (cf. commentaries and lexicons). LXX, Vulgate, Targum, and Syriac all translated "angels"; Aquila, Symmachus, and Theodotion translated "God." AV and JPS have "angels."
[4] "And didst set him over the works of thy hands": these words are omitted by the Greek texts
of Tischendorf, Nestle, Vogels, Merk, Bover, Bible Societies; included by <u>Textus Receptus</u>,
Westcott and Hort (in brackets), Soden, Souter.

Harden not your hearts, as in the provocation,
Like as in the day of the temptation in the
wilderness,
Wherewith your fathers tempted me by prov-
ing me
And saw my works forty years.
Wherefore I was displeased with this genera-
tion,
And said, They do always err in their heart:
But they did not know my ways;
As I sware in my wrath,
They shall not enter into my rest.

Harden not your hearts, as in the provoca-
tion,[5]
Like as in the day of the temptation[6] in the
wilderness,
Where your fathers tempted me,
They proved me and saw my works.
Forty years I was displeased with this genera-
tion,
And said, They do always err in their heart:
And they did not know my ways;
As I sware in my wrath,
They shall not enter into my rest.

MT Psa 95.7-11
Today, *Oh that ye would hear* his voice!
Harden not your heart, as at Meribah,
As in the day of Massah in the wilderness:
When your fathers tempted me,
Proved me, and saw my work.
Forty years long was I grieved with that
generation,
And said, It is a people that do err in their
heart,
And they have not known my ways:
Wherefore I sware in my wrath,
That they should not enter into my rest.

3.15 (cf. 3.7-8a)
Today if ye shall hear his voice,
Harden not your hearts, as in the provocation.

LXX Psa 94.7-8
Today if ye shall hear his voice,
Harden not your hearts, as in the provoca-
tion.[7]

MT Psa 95.7-8
Today, *Oh that ye would hear* his voice!
Harden not your heart, as at Meribah.

3.18 (A) (cf. 3.11)
And to whom sware he that they should not
enter into his rest . . . ?

LXX Psa 94.11
As I sware in my wrath,
They shall not enter into my rest.

MT Psa 95.11
Wherefore I sware in my wrath,
That they should not enter into my rest.

4.3 (cf. 3.11)
As I sware in my wrath,
They shall not enter into my rest.

LXX Psa 94.11
As I sware in my wrath,
They shall not enter into my rest.

---

[5] "Provocation": MT m^{e}rĩbā(h) "strife" (cf. Exo 17.7; Num 20.13).
[6] "Temptation": MT massā(h) "tempting" (cf. Exo 17.7).
[7] "Provocation": MT m^{e}rĩbā(h) "strife" (cf. Exo 17.7; Num 20.13).

MT Psa 95.11
Wherefore I sware in my wrath,
That they should not enter into my rest.

4.4
And God rested on the seventh day from all his works.

LXX Gen 2.2
And God . . . rested on the seventh day from all his works.

MT
And he rested on the seventh day from all his *work.*

4.5 (cf. 3.11)
They shall not enter into my rest

LXX Psa 94.11b
They shall not enter into my rest.

MT Psa 95.11b
That they should not enter into my rest.

4.7 (cf. 3.7-8)
Today if ye shall hear his voice,
Harden not your hearts.

LXX Psa 94.7-8
Today if ye shall hear his voice,
Harden not your hearts . . .

MT Psa 95.7-8
Today, *Oh that ye would hear* his voice!
Harden not your heart . . .

4.10 (A) (cf. 4.4-5)
For he that is entered into his rest hath himself also rested from his works, as God did from his.

LXX Psa 94.11 and Gen 2.2
. . . They shall not enter into my rest.
And God . . . rested on the seventh day from all his works.

5.5 (cf. 1.5)
Thou art my Son,
This day have I begotten thee.

Psa 2.7
Thou art my son;
This day have I begotten thee.

5.6
Thou art a priest for ever
After the order of Melchizedek.

Psa 110.4
Thou art a priest for ever
After the order of Melchizedek.

6.8 (A)
But if it beareth thorns and thistles, it is rejected and nigh unto a curse . . .

Gen 3.17-18
. . . cursed is the ground for thy sake . . .
thorns also and thistles shall it bring forth to thee . . .

[65]

Hebrews

6.13-14	Gen 22.16-17

6.13-14
. . . *God* . . . sware by himself, saying, Surely
blessing I will bless thee, and multiplying I will
multiply *thee.*

Gen 22.16-17
By myself have I sworn, saith *the Lord* . . .
that in blessing I will bless them, and in multiplying I will multiply *thy seed* . . .

6.19 (A)
. . . entering into that which is within the
    veil . . .

Lev 16.12 (cf. 16.2)
. . . and (he shall) bring it within the veil . . .

7.1-2 (P)
For this Melchizedek, king of Salem, priest of
God Most High, who met Abraham returning
from the slaughter of the kings, and blessed
him, to whom also Abraham divided a tenth
part of all . . .

Gen 14.17-20
And the king of Sodom went out to meet him,
after his return from the slaughter of Chedor-
laomer and the kings that were with him
. . . And Melchizedek king of Salem brought
forth bread and wine: and he was priest of God
Most High. And he blessed him . . . And he
gave him a tenth of all.

7.17 (cf. 5.6)
Thou art a priest for ever
After the order of Melchizedek.

Psa 110.4
Thou art a priest for ever.
After the order of Melchizedek.

7.21 (cf. 5.6)
The Lord sware and will not repent himself,
Thou art a priest for ever.

Psa 110.4
The Lord hath sworn, and will not repent,
Thou art a priest for ever.

8.1 (A) (cf. 1.13)
. . . who sat down on the right hand of the
throne of the Majesty . . .

Psa 110.1
Sit thou at my right hand . . .

8.5
See, saith he, that thou make *all things* according to the pattern that was shewed thee in
the mount.

LXX Exo 25.40
See that thou make *them* according to the
pattern that was shewed thee in the mount.

MT
And see that thou make *them* after *their*
pattern, which hath been shewed thee in the
mount.

8.8-12
Behold, the days come, saith the Lord,
That I will make a new covenant with the
    house of Israel and with the house of
    Judah;

LXX Jer 38.31-34
Behold, the days come, saith the Lord,
That I will make[8] a new covenant with the
    house of Israel and with the house of
    Judah;

Not according to the covenant that I *made*
    with their fathers
In the day that I took them by the hand to lead
    them forth out of the land of Egypt;
For they continued not in my covenant,
And I regarded them not, saith the Lord.
For this is the covenant that I will make with
    the house of Israel
After those days, saith the Lord;
I will put my laws into their mind,
And on their heart also will I write them:
And I will be to them a God,
And they shall be to me a people:
And they shall not teach every man his fellow-
    citizen,
And every man his brother, saying, Know the
    Lord:
For all shall know me,
From the least to the greatest of them.
For I will be merciful to their iniquities,
And their sins will I remember no more.

Not according to the covenant which I *cove-*
    nanted with their fathers
In the day that I took them by the hand to lead
    them forth out of the land of Egypt;
For they continued not in my covenant,
And I regarded them not, saith the Lord.
For this is the covenant that I will make with
    the house of Israel
After those days, saith the Lord;
I will put my laws into their mind,
And on their heart also will I write them:
And I will be to them a God,
And they shall be to me a people:
And they shall not teach every man his fellow-
    citizen,
And every man his brother, saying, Know the
    Lord:
For all shall know me,
From the least of them even to the greatest of
    them.
For I will be merciful to their iniquities,
And their sins will I remember no more.

MT Jer 31.31-34
Behold, the days come, saith the Lord,
That I will make a new covenant with the
    house of Israel and with the house of
    Judah:
Not according to the covenant that I made
    with their fathers
In the day that I took them by the hand to
    bring them out of the land of Egypt;
Which my covenant they brake, although I was
    an husband unto them, saith the Lord.
But this is the covenant that I will make with
    the house of Israel
After those days, saith the Lord;
I will put my law in their *inward parts*,
And in their heart will I write it;
And I will be their God,
And they shall be my people:
And they shall teach no more every man his
    neighbour,
And every man his brother, saying, Know the
    Lord:
For they shall all know me,
From the least of them unto the greatest of
    them, saith the Lord:
For I will *forgive their iniquity*,
And their *sin* will I remember no more.

---

[8] "Make": LXX diathēsomai "I will covenant"; N.T. suntelesō "I will complete."

Hebrews

9.20
This is the blood of the covenant which *God commanded to you-ward.* ·

Exo 24.8
Behold the blood of the covenant which *the Lord hath made with* you concerning all these words.

9.28 (A)
... to bear the sins of many ...

Isa 53.12
... he bare the sins of many ...

10.5-7 (cf. vv. 8, 9, 10)
Sacrifice and offering thou wouldest not,
But a body didst thou prepare for me;
In whole burnt offerings and sacrifices for sin
    thou hadst no pleasure:
Then said I, Lo, I am come
(In the roll of the book it is written of me)
To do thy will, O God.

LXX Psa 39.7-9
Sacrifice and offering thou wouldest not,
But a body[9] didst thou prepare for me;
Whole burnt offering and sacrifice for sin *thou
    didst not desire:*
Then said I, Lo, I am come
(In the roll of the book it is written of me).
To do thy will, O my God, I desired,
And thy law is within my heart.

MT Psa 40.6-8
Sacrifice and offering thou *hast no delight in;*
Mine ears hast thou opened:
Burnt offering and sin offering *hast thou not
    required.*
Then said I, Lo, I am come;
In the roll of the book it is written of me:
I delight to do thy will, O my God;
Yea, thy law is within my heart.

10.12-13 (A) (cf. 1.13)
... he sat down on the right hand of God;
from henceforth expecting till his enemies be
made the footstool of his feet.

Psa 110.1
Sit thou at my right hand,
Until I make thine enemies thy footstool.

10.16-17 (cf. 8.10, 12)
This is the covenant that I will make with
    them
After those days, saith the Lord;
I will put my laws on their heart,
And upon their mind also will I write them;
And their sins and their iniquities will I re-
    member no more.

LXX Jer 38.33, 34
For this is the covenant that I will make with
    the house of Israel
After those days, saith the Lord;
I will put my laws into their mind,
And on their heart also will I write them;
... And their sins will I remember no more.

MT Jer 31.33-34
But this is the covenant that I will make with
    the house of Israel
After those days, saith the Lord;
I will put my law in their *inward parts.*

---

[9] "Body": sōma is the reading of mss. B, Aleph, A, of the LXX; ms. G reads ōtia "ears" (in
accordance with the MT), and this reading is preferred by Rahlfs (Swete prefers sōma).

And in their heart will I write it . . .
. . . and their *sin* will I remember no more.

10.27 (A)
. . . a fierceness[10] of fire which shall devour
the adversaries.

LXX Isa 26.11
. . . Fury[11] shall overtake an undisciplined
people, and now fire shall devour the adversaries.

MT
. . . But they shall see thy zeal for the people,
and be ashamed; yea, fire shall devour thine
adversaries.

10.28 (A)
A man that hath set at nought Moses' law
dieth without compassion on the word of two
or three witnesses.

Deut 17.6
At the mouth of two witnesses, or three
witnesses, shall he that is to die be put to
death . . .

10.30a (cf. Rom 12.19)
Vengeance belongeth unto me, I will recompense.

Deut 32.35
MT: Vengeance is mine, and recompense . . .
LXX: In the day of vengeance I will recom-
pense . . .

10.30b
The Lord shall judge his people.

Deut 32.36 (cf. Psa 135.14)
For the Lord shall judge his people . . .

10.37-38
For yet a very little while,[12]
He that cometh shall come, and shall not
tarry.
But *my* righteous one shall live by faith.[13]
And if *he* shrink back, my soul hath no pleas-
ure *in him.*

LXX Hab 2.3-4
. . . If the vision delay, wait for it,
For *it* shall *surely* come, and shall not tarry.
If *it* shrink back, my soul hath no pleasure in
it:
But *the* righteous one shall live by *my* faith.[14]

MT
. . . Though (the vision) tarry, wait for it;
because it will *surely* come, *it* will not delay.
Behold, his soul is puffed up, it is not upright
in him: but the just shall live by his faith.

---

[10] "Fierceness": Gk. zēlos "zeal," "fury," corresponding to the LXX wording.
[11] "Fury": or "zeal"; Gk. zēlos.
[12] Cf. LXX Isaiah 26.20: "A very little while."
[13] Cf. Romans 1.17.
[14] "Faith": or "faithfulness"; the Gk. pistis translates the Heb. 'ĕmūnā(h) (cf. Koehler).

Hebrews

11.5 (P)
. . . Enoch . . . was not found, because God translated him . . . he had been well-pleasing unto God.

LXX Gen 5.24
And Enoch pleased God, and he was not found, because God translated him.

MT
And Enoch walked with God: and he was not; for God took him.

11.12 (A)
. . . as the stars of heaven in multitude, and as the sand, which is by the sea shore, innumerable.

Gen 22.17 (cf. 15.5)
. . . as the stars of the heaven, and as the sand which is upon the sea shore . . .

11.18
In Isaac shall thy seed be called.

Gen 21.12
. . . For in Isaac shall thy seed be called.

11.21
. . . Jacob . . . worshipped, leaning upon the top of his staff.

LXX Gen 47.31
. . . and Israel worshipped upon the top of his staff.

MT
And Israel bowed himself upon the bed's head.

12.2 (A) (cf. 1.13)
. . . he hath sat down at the right hand of the throne of God.

Psa 110.1
Sit thou at my right hand . . .

12.5-6
My son, regard not lightly the chastening of the Lord,
Nor faint when thou art reproved of him;
For whom the Lord loveth he chasteneth,
And scourgeth every son whom he receiveth.

LXX Prov 3.11-12
Son, regard not lightly the chastening of the Lord,
Nor faint when thou art reproved of him;
For whom the Lord loveth he chasteneth,
And scourgeth every son whom he receiveth.

MT
My son, despise not the chastening of the Lord;
Neither *be weary* of his reproof:
For whom the Lord loveth he reproveth;
Even as a father the son in whom *he delight-eth.*

12.12-13 (A)
Wherefore lift up the hands that hang down, and the palsied knees; and make straight paths for your[15] feet . . .

LXX Isa 35.3 and Prov 4.26
Be strong, O ye hands that hang idle and knees that are palsied.
Make thou straight paths for thy feet . . .

MT
Strengthen ye the weak hands, and confirm the
feeble knees.
Make level the path of thy feet . . .

12.15 (A)
. . . lest any root of bitterness springing up
trouble[16] you . . .

LXX Deut 29.17
Is there among you any root springing up in
gall[17] and bitterness?

MT
. . . lest there should be among you a root that
beareth gall and wormwood.

12.20 (P)
If even a beast touch the moutain, it shall be
stoned.

Exo 19.12-13
. . . Whosoever toucheth the mount . . . shall
surely be stoned, or shot through; whether it
be beast or man, it shall not live . . .

12.21
I exceedingly fear and quake . . .

Deut 9.19
For I was afraid . . .

12.26
Yet once more will I make to tremble not the
earth only, but also the heaven.

LXX Hag 2.6
Yet once more I will make to tremble the
heaven and the earth and the sea and the dry
land.

MT
Yet once, it is a little while, and I will shake
the heavens, and the earth, and the sea, and
the dry land.

12.29 (A)
For our God is a consuming fire.

Deut 4.24
For the Lord thy God is a devouring fire, a
jealous God.

13.5
I will in no wise fail thee, neither will I in any
wise forsake thee.

LXX Deut 31.6 (cf. 31.8; Josh 1.5)
For the Lord thy God . . . will in no wise fail
thee, neither will he forsake thee.

---

[15] "Your" is plural; in the LXX "thy" is singular.

[16] "Trouble": Gk. enochlē.

[17] "In gall": Gk. en cholē.

MT
For *the Lord thy God* . . . will not fail thee,
nor forsake thee.

13.6
The Lord is my helper; I will not fear:
What shall man do unto me?

LXX Psa 117.6
The Lord is my helper, I will not fear
what man shall do unto me.[18]

MT Psa 118.6
The Lord is *on my side*; I will not fear:
what can man do unto me?

13.11 (A)
For the bodies of those beasts, whose blood is
brought into the holy place . . . as an offering
for sin, are burned without the camp.

Lev 16.27
And the bullock of the sin offering, and the
goat of the sin offering, whose blood was
brought in . . . the holy place, shall be carried

forth without the camp; and they shall burn in
the fire . . .

James

James

Old Testament

1.10-11 (A) (cf. 1 Pet 1.24-25)
. . . as the flower of the grass he shall pass
away.
For the sun ariseth . . . and withereth the
grass; and the flower thereof falleth . . .

LXX Isa 40.6-7
. . . All flesh is grass, and all the glory of man
as the flower of the grass: the grass withereth,
and the flower falleth . . .

MT
. . . All flesh is grass, and all the goodliness
thereof is as the flower of the field: the grass
withereth, the flower fadeth . . .

2.8 (cf. Mt 19.19)
Thou shalt love thy neighbor as thyself.

Lev 19.18
Thou shalt love thy neighbor as thyself.

2.11 (cf. Mt 5.27, 21)
Do not commit adultery . . . Do not kill.[1]

Exo 20.14, 13 (cf. Deut 5.18, 17)
Thou shalt not commit adultery . . . Thou shalt
do no murder

---

[18] The punctuation of the LXX text follows Rahlfs.
[1] "Kill": the Gk. phoneuō may also mean "to murder."

2.21 (A)	Gen 22.9
Abraham . . . offered up Isaac his son upon the altar.	. . . And Abraham built the altar . . and bound Isaac his son, and laid him on the altar . . .

2.23a (cf. Rom 4.3)	LXX Gen 15.6
And Abraham believed God, and it was reckoned unto him for righteousness.	And Abraham believed God, and it was reckoned unto him for righteousness.
	MT
	And he believed *in the Lord;* and *he counted it to him* for righteousness.

2.23b (A)	Isa 41.8
. . . He was called the friend of God.	. . . Abraham my friend.

3.9 (A)	Gen 1.26
. . . men . . . are made after the likeness of God.	And God said, Let us make man in our image, after our likeness . . .

4.5	No O.T. passage.[3]
He yearns jealously over the spirit which he has made to dwell in us.[2]	

4.6 (1 Peter 5.5)	LXX Prov 3.34
God resisteth the proud, but giveth grace to the humble.	*The Lord* resisteth the proud, but giveth grace to the humble.
	MT
	Surely *he scorneth the scorners,* But he giveth grace unto the lowly.

5.4 (A)	LXX Isa 5.9
. . . the cries of them that reaped[4] have entered into the ears of the Lord of Sabaoth.	For these things were heard in the ears of the Lord of Sabaoth.

---

[2] RSV; ERV punctuates the verse in such a way as to avoid a quotation: "Doth the spirit which he made to dwell in us long unto envying?" (but cf. ERV footnote). The majority of editions of the Greek text punctuate the verse as does RSV. There is much disagreement over the actual meaning of the statement (cf. commentaries).

[3] There is no single O.T. passage which corresponds to the quotation. Commentators suggest various passages which seem to them to contain the thought expressed in the N.T. quotation.

[4] Cf. Deut 24.15: "In his day thou shalt give him his hire . . . lest he cry against thee unto the Lord . . . ."

MT
In mine ears saith the Lord of hosts . . .

5.11 (A)
. . . the Lord is full of pity, and merciful.

Psa 103.8
The Lord is full of compassion . . . and plenteous in mercy.

1 Peter

1 Peter

Old Testament

1.16
Ye shall be holy; for I am holy.

Lev 19.2 (cf. 11.44; 20.7)
Ye shall be holy: for I the Lord your God am holy.

1.24-25 (cf. Jas 1.10-11)
All flesh is as grass,
And all the glory thereof as the flower of grass.
The grass withereth, and the flower falleth:
But the word of the Lord abideth for ever.

LXX Isa 40.6-8
All flesh is grass,
And all the glory of man as the flower of grass.
The grass withereth, and the flower falleth:
But the word of our God abideth for ever.

MT
All flesh is grass, and all the goodliness thereof is as the flower of the field: . . .
The grass withereth, the flower fadeth:
But the word of our God shall stand for ever.

2.3 (A)
If ye have tasted that the Lord is gracious.

LXX Psa 33.9
Taste ye and see that the Lord is gracious.

MT Psa 34.8
O taste and see that the Lord is good.

2.6 (cf. Rom 9.33)
Behold, I lay in Zion a chief corner stone, elect, precious:
And he that believeth on him shall not be put to shame.

LXX Isa 28.16
Behold, I place in the foundations of Zion a chief corner stone, costly, elect, precious . . .
And he that believeth on him shall not be put to shame.

MT
Behold, I lay in Zion for a foundation a stone, a tried stone, a precious corner stone . . .
He that believeth shall not make haste.

2.7 (cf. Mt 21.42)
The stone which the builders rejected,
The same was made the head of the corner.

Psa 118.22
The stone which the builders rejected,
Is become the head of the corner.

2.8 (cf. Rom 9.33)
A stone of stumbling, and a rock of offence.

Isa 8.14
But for a stone for stumbling and for a rock of offence . . .

2.9 (A)

But ye are an elect race, a royal priesthood, a holy nation, a people for God's own possession, that ye may shew forth the excellencies of him who called you . . .

LXX Exo 23.22 (cf. Exo 19.5-6) and Isa 43.20-21
If ye shall indeed hear my voice . . . ye shall
    be to me a people of my own possession
    . . . a royal priesthood and a holy nation.
. . . My elect race, my people whom I pos-
    sessed for myself to proclaim my excel-
    lencies.

MT Exo 19.5-6
. . . Ye shall be a peculiar treasure unto me
    from among all peoples . . . and ye shall
    be unto me a kingdom of priests, and an
    holy nation.
Isa 43.20-21
. . . my people, my chosen: the people which I
    formed for myself, that they might set
    forth my praise.

2.10 (A) (cf. Rom 9.25-26)
Which in time past were no people, but now are the people of God: which had not obtained mercy, but now have obtained mercy.

LXX Hos 1.6, 9; 2.1, 23
Call thou her name, She-obtained-not-
    mercy . . .
Call thou his name, Not-my-people . . .

Say ye to your brother, My-people, and to your
    sister, She-obtained-mercy.
. . . And I will have mercy on She-obtained-
    not-mercy, and I will say to Not-my-
    people, Thou art my people . . .

MT
Call her name Lo-ruhamah: for I will no more
    have mercy upon the house of Israel . . .
Call his name Lo-ammi: for ye are not my
    people . . .
Say ye unto your brethren, Ammi; and to your
    sisters, Ruhamah.
. . . and I will have mercy upon her that had
    not obtained mercy; and I will say to
    them which were not my people, Thou
    art my people . . .

1 Peter

2.22 (A)
Who did no sin, neither was guile found in his
mouth.

LXX Isa 53.9
. . . For he did no iniquity, neither was guile
found in his mouth.

MT
. . . although he had done no violence, neither
was any deceit in his mouth.

2.24-25 (A)
Who his own self bare our sins . . . by whose
stripes ye were healed. For ye were going
astray like sheep . . .

LXX Isa 53.4-6 (cf. 53.12)
He bares our sins . . . by his stripes we were
    healed.
For we all like sheep went astray . . .

MT
Surely he hath borne our griefs . . . with his
stripes we are healed. All we like sheep have
gone astray . . .

3.6 (A)
As Sarah obeyed Abraham, calling him
lord . . .

Gen 18.12
And Sarah laughed within herself, saying . . .
My lord being old also?

3.10-12
He that *would love* life,
And see good days,
Let *him* refrain his tongue from evil,
And *his* lips that they speak no guile:
And let *him* turn away from evil, and do good;
Let *him* seek peace, and pursue it.
For the eyes of the Lord are upon the right-
eous,
And his ears unto their supplication:
But the face of the Lord is upon them that do
    evil.

LXX Psa 33.13-17
Who is the man who *wishes* life,
Who loves to see good days?
Refrain *thy* tongue from evil,
And *thy* lips that they speak no guile:
Turn *thou* away from evil, and do good,
Seek peace, and pursue it.
The eyes of the Lord are upon the righteous,
And his ears unto their supplication:
But the face of the Lord is upon them that do
    evil . . .

MT Psa 34.12-16
What man is he that *desireth* life,
And loveth many *days, that he may see good?*
Keep *thy* tongue from evil,
And *thy* lips from speaking guile.
Depart from evil, and do good;
Seek peace, and pursue it.
The eyes of the Lord are toward the righteous,
And his ears are open unto their cry.
The face of the Lord is against them that do
    evil . . .

3.14-15 (A)
. . . And fear not their fear, neither be
troubled; but sanctify in your hearts Christ as
Lord . . .

Isa 8.12-13
. . . Neither fear ye their fear, nor be ye in
dread thereof. The Lord of hosts, him shall ye
sanctify . . .

4.8 (A)
... For love covereth a multitude of sins.

Prov 10.12
... But love covereth all transgressions.

4.14 (A)
... the Spirit of God resteth upon you.

LXX Isa 11.2
... and the Spirit of God shall rest upon him.

MT
... and the spirit of the Lord shall rest upon him.

4.18
And if the righteous is scarcely saved, where shall the ungodly and sinner appear?

LXX Prov 11.31
If indeed the righteous is scarcely saved, where shall the ungodly and sinner appear?

MT
Behold, the righteous shall be recompensed in the earth:
How much more the wicked and the sinner!

5.5 (cf. Jas 4.6)
... For God resisteth the proud, but giveth grace to the humble.

LXX Prov 3.34
The Lord resisteth the proud, but giveth grace to the humble.

MT
Surely he scorneth the scorners,
But he giveth grace unto the lowly.

5.7 (A)
Casting all your[1] anxiety upon him ...

LXX Psa 54.23
Cast all thy anxiety upon the Lord ...

MT Psa 55.22
Cast thy burden upon the Lord ...

2 Peter

2 Peter

Old Testament

1.17 (A) (cf. Mt 17.5)
This is my beloved Son, in whom I am well pleased.

Psa 2.7: Thou art my son ...
Gen 22.2: ... thine only[2] son, whom thou lovest ...
Isa 42.1: ... my chosen, in whom my soul delighteth ...

---

[1] "Your": pl. in N.T.; "thy" sg. in LXX.
[2] "Only": Heb. et-yᵉḥⁱdᵉkā; LXX ton agapēton "the beloved"; in certain contexts the Gk. ho agapētos means "only."

2.22	Prov 26.11
The dog returning to his own vomit again . . .	As a dog that returneth to his vomit . . .

3.8 (A)	Psa 90.4
. . . one day is with the Lord as a thousand years, and a thousand years as one day.	For a thousand years in thy sight are but as yesterday when it is past . . .

3.13 (A)	Isa 65.17 (cf. 66.22)
But, according to his promise, we look for new heavens and a new earth . . .	For, behold, I create new heavens and a new earth.

Jude

Jude	Old Testament
9 (A)	Zech 3.2
But Michael the archangel, when contending with the devil he disputed about the body of Moses, durst not bring against him a railing judgement, but said, The Lord rebuke thee.[1]	And the Lord said unto Satan, The Lord rebuke thee, O Satan . . .

14-15	1 Enoch 1.9; 5.4; 60.8[2]
And to these also Enoch, the seventh from Adam, prophesied, saying, Behold the Lord came with ten thousands of his holy ones, to execute judgement upon all and to convict all the ungodly of all their works of ungodliness which they have ungodly wrought, and of all the hard things which ungodly sinners have	60.8: . . . the seventh from Adam . . . 1.9: And lo! He comes with ten thousands of his holy ones to execute judgment upon them, and He will destroy the ungodly and will convict all flesh of all that the sinners and ungodly have wrought and ungodly committed against him. 5.4: But ye have turned away and spoken proud and hard words with your impure mouths against His greatness.

---

[1] The account of Michael's disputing with the devil over the body of Moses is taken from The Assumption of Moses, a Jewish apocryphal work of the 1st century A.D. Though this particular section of the work has not yet been recovered, several early Christian Fathers, including Clement of Alexandria and Origen, expressly declare this work to have been the source of the allusion by Jude (cf. commentaries, and R.H. Charles The Apocrypha and Pseudepigrapha of the Old Testament, vol. II, pp. 407-424). Charles sees also the influence of the Testament of Moses in v. 16.

[2] These excerpts from 1 Enoch are translations from the Ethiopic (by Charles); the surviving Greek copies differ somewhat (cf. commentaries, and Charles, op. cit., pp. 163-187). Further influence of 1 Enoch in Jude is seen in vv. 6 and 13.

Revelation

Revelation

Old Testament

1.7a (A) (cf. Mt 24.30b)
Behold, he cometh with the clouds . . .

Dan 7.13
. . . behold, there came with the clouds of
heaven one like unto a son of man . . .

1.7b (A) (cf. Jn 19.37)
. . . and every eye shall see him, and they
which pierced him; and all the tribes of the
earth shall mourn over him.

Zech 12.10
. . . and they shall look unto me whom they
have pierced: and they shall mourn for him . . .

2.26-27 (A)
. . . to him will I give authority over the
nations: and he shall rule them with a rod of
iron, as the vessels of the potter are broken to
shivers . . .

LXX Psa 2.8-9
Ask of me, and I will give thee the nations for
    thine inheritance,
And the ends of the earth for thy possession.
Thou shalt rule them with a rod of iron,
As the potter's vessel thou shalt break them to
    shivers.

MT
Ask of me, and I will give thee the nations for ·
    thine inheritance,
And the uttermost parts of the earth for thy
    possession.
Thou shalt break them with a rod of iron,
Thou shalt dash them in pieces like a potter's
    vessel.

3.7 (A)
. . . he that hath the key of David, he that
openeth, and none shall shut, and that
shutteth, and none openeth.

Isa 22.22
And the key of the house of David will I lay
upon his shoulder; and he shall open, and none
shall shut; and he shall shut, and none shall
open.

3.19 (A) (cf. Heb 12.6)
As many as I love, I reprove and chasten . . .

LXX Prov 3.12
For whom the Lord loveth he chasteneth,
And scourgeth every son whom he receiveth.

MT
For whom the Lord loveth he reproveth:
Even as a father the son in whom he delight-
    eth.

Revelation

4.8 (A) Holy, holy, holy, is the Lord God, the Almighty . . .	Isa 6.3 Holy, holy, holy, is the Lord of hosts . . .

6.16 (A) (cf. Lk 23.30) And they say to the mountains and *to the* rocks, Fall on us, and hide us . . .	Hos 10.8 . . . And they shall say to the mountains, Cover us; and to the hills, Fall on us.

9.20 (A) . . . The idols of gold, and of silver, and of brass and of stone, and of wood; which can neither see, nor hear, nor walk.	Dan 5.23 (cf. Psa 115.4-7; 135.15-17) . . . the gods of silver, and gold, of brass, iron, wood and stone, which see not, nor hear, nor know . . .

10.6 (A) (cf. Acts 4.24) . . . who created the heaven and the things that are therein, and the earth and the things that are therein, and the sea and the things that are therein . . .	Exo 20.11 (cf. Psa 146.6) . . . The Lord made heaven and earth, the sea, and all that in them is . . .

13.7 (A) And it was given unto him to make war with the saints, and to overcome them . . .	Dan 7.21 I beheld, and the same horn made war with the saints, and prevailed against them.

14.7 (A) (cf. 10.6) . . . and worship him that made the heaven and the earth and sea and fountains of waters.	Exo 20.11 (cf. Psa 146.6) . . . The Lord made heaven and earth, the sea . . .

APPENDIX

The Quotations in the Order of the Old Testament

As in the main list, "(A)" designates allusions, while "(P)" designates paraphrases.

GENESIS

1.26	James 3.9 (A)
1.27	Matt 19.4 (P); Mark 10.6 (P)
2.2	Heb 4.4,10 (A); 6.8
2.7	1 Cor 15.45 (P); 15.47 (A)
2.24	Matt 19.5; Mark 10.7-8; 1 Cor 6.16; Eph 5.31
3.17-18	Heb 6.8 (A)
5.2	Matt 19.4 (P); Mark 10.6
5.24	Heb 11.5 (P)
12.1	Acts 7.3
12.3	Acts 3.25; Gal 3.8
12.17	Gal 3.16
13.15	Gal 3.16
14.17-20	Heb 7.1-2 (P)
15.5	Rom 4.18; Heb 11.12 (A)
15.6	Rom 4.3,9,22 (A); Gal 3.6; James 2.23a
15.13	Acts 7.6 (P)
15.14	Acts 7.7 (P)
17.5	Rom 4.17,18a
17.7	Gal 3.16
17.8	Acts 7.5 (P); Gal 3.16
18.10	Rom 9.9
18.12	1 Peter 3.6 (A)
18.18	Acts 3.25; Gal 3.8
21.10	Gal 4.30
21.12	Rom 9.7; Heb 11.18
22.2	Matt 3.17 (A); 17.5 (A); Mark 1.11 (A); 9.7 (A); Luke 3.22 (A); 9.35; 2 Peter 1.17 (A)
22.9	James 2.21 (A)
22.16-17	Heb 6.13-14
22.17	Heb 11.12 (A)
22.18	Acts 3.25; Gal 3.8
24.7	Gal 3.16
25.23	Rom 9.12
26.4	Acts 3.25; Gal 3.8
28.4	Acts 3.25; Gal 3.8
28.12	John 1.51 (A)
28.14	Acts 3.25; Gal 3.8
46.27	Acts 7.14 (A)
47.31	Heb 11.21

EXODUS

1.51	Acts 7.14 (A)
1.8	Acts 7.18
2.13-15	Acts 7.27-29 (P)

2.14	Acts 7.35	32.6	1 Cor 10.7	
3.5,7,8a,10a	Acts 7.33-34 (P)	32.23	Acts 7.40	
3.6	Matt 22.32; Mark 12.26; Luke 20.37 (P); Acts 3.13; 7.32	33.19	Rom 9.15	
		34.33	2 Cor 3.13 (A)	
3.12	Acts 7.7 (P)	34.34	2 Cor 3.16 (A)	
3.15	Matt 22.32; Mark 12.26; Luke 20.37 (P); Acts 3.13 (A); 7.32	34.35	2 Cor 3.7 (A), 13 (A)	
9.16	Rom 9.17		**LEVITICUS**	
12.46	John 19.36	11.44	1 Peter 1.16	
13.2	Luke 2.23 (P)	12.8	Luke 2.24	
13.12,15	Luke 2.23 (P)	16.2	Heb 6.19 (A)	
16.4,15	John 6.31 (P)	16.12	Heb 6.19 (A)	
16.18	2 Cor 8.15	16.27	Heb 13.11 (A)	
19.5-6	1 Peter 2.9 (A)	18.5	Rom 10.5 (P); Gal 3.12	
19.12-13	Heb 12.20 (P)	19.2	1 Peter 1.16	
20.11	Acts 4.24 (A); 14.15 (A); Rev 10.6 (A); 14.7	19.12	Matt 5.33 (P)	
		19.18	Matt 5.43; 19.19; 22.39; Mark 12.31-33; Luke 10.27; Rom 13.9b; Gal 5.14; James 2.8	
20.12-16	Matt 5.21,27,43; 19.18-19; Mark 10.19; Luke 18.20			
20.12	Matt 15.4a; 19.19; Mark 7.10a; 10.19; Luke 18.20; Eph 6.2-3	20.7	1 Peter 1.16	
		24.20	Matt 5.38	
20.13	Matt 5.21; 19.18; Mark 10.19; Luke 18.20; Rom 13.9; James 2.11	26.12	2 Cor 6.16 (P)	
			NUMBERS	
20.13-15,17	Matt 19.18; Rom 13.9a	9.12	John 19.36	
20.14	Matt 5.27; 19.18; Mark 10.19; Luke 18.20; Rom 13.9; James 2.11	12.7	Heb 3.2,5 (A)	
		14.16	1 Cor 10.5 (A)	
		16.5	2 Tim 2.19 (A)	
20.17	Rom 7.7; 13.9	27.17	Mark 6.34 (A)	
21.17	Matt 15.4b; Mark 7.10b	30.2	Matt 5.33 (P)	
21.24	Matt 5.38			
22.28	Acts 23.5		**DEUTERONOMY**	
23.22	1 Peter 2.9 (A)	1.31	Acts 13.18 (A)	
24.8	Heb 9.20	4.24	Heb 12.29 (A)	
25.40	Heb 8.5	4.35	Mark 12.32-33 (P)	
32.1	Acts 7.40	5.5,17,19,21	Matt 19.18; Rom 13.9a	

5.16	Matt 15.4a; 19.19; Mark 7.10a; 10.19; Luke 18.20; Eph 6.2-3	25.5	Matt 22.24 (P); Mark 12.19 (P); Luke 20.28 (P)
5.16-20	Matt 5.21,27,43; 19.18-19	27.26	Gal 3.10
5.17	Matt 5.21; 19.18; Mark 10.19; Luke 18.20; Rom 13.9; James 2.11	29.4	Rom 11.8
		29.18	Heb 12.15 (A)
		30.12-14	Rom 10.6-8 (P)
5.18	Matt 5.27; 19.18; Mark 10.19; Luke 18.20; Rom 13.9; James 2.11	31.6-8	Heb 13.5
		32.17	1 Cor 10.20 (A)
		32.21	Rom 10.19; 1 Cor 10.22 (A)
5.21	Rom 7.7; 13.9	32.35	Rom 12.19; Heb 10.30a
6.4-5	Mark 12.29-30; 12.32-33 (P)	32.36	Heb 10.30b
6.5	Matt 22.37; Mark 12.29-30; Luke 10.27	32.43	Rom 15.10; Heb 1.6
6.13	Matt 4.10; Luke 4.8		JOSHUA
6.16	Matt 4.7; Luke 4.12	1.5	Heb 13.5
7.1	Acts 13.19 (P)		
8.3	Matt 4.4; Luke 4.4		1 SAMUEL
9.4	Rom 10.6-8 (P)	1.11	Luke 1.48 (A)
9.19	Heb 12.21	2.26	Luke 2.52 (A)
14.2	Titus 2.14 (A)	12.22 (12.12)	Rom 11.2 (A)
17.6	Heb 10.28 (A)	13.14	Acts 13.22 (P)
17.7	1 Cor 5.13 (P)		
18.15	Matt 17.5 (A); Mark 9.7 (A); Luke 9.35 (A); Acts 3.22; 7.37		2 SAMUEL
18.15-16	Acts 3.22-23; 7.37	7.8,14	2 Cor 6.18 (P)
19.15	Matt 18.16 (A); John 8.17; 2 Cor 13.1 (A); 1 Tim 5.19 (A)	7.12-13	Acts 2.30 (P)
		7.14	2 Cor 6.18 (P); Heb 1.5
		22.3	Heb 2.13a
19.19	1 Cor 5.13 (P)	22.50	Rom 15.9
19.21	Matt 5.38		
21.23	Gal 3.13		1 KINGS
22.24	1 Cor 5.13 (P)	2.10	Acts 13.36 (P)
24.1	Matt 5.31 (P); 19.7 (P); Mark 10.4 (P)	19.10	Rom 11.3
		19.14	Rom 11.3
24.7	1 Cor 5.13 (P)	19.18	Rom 11.4
25.4	1 Cor 9.9; 1 Tim 5.18a	22.17	Mark 6.34 (A)

2 KINGS

1.10	Luke 9.54 (A)
1.12	Luke 9.54 (A)

NEHEMIAH

9.15	John 6.3 (P)

JOB

5.13	1 Cor 3.19
13.16	Phil 1.19 (A)
41.11	Rom 11.35

PSALMS

Modern translations of the Book of Psalms use a variety of systems of chapter and verse numbering. In this list, the basic reference indicates the LXX (Septuagint) system, while the reference in parentheses indicates that of the ERV (English Revised Version).

2.1-2	Acts 4.25-26
2.7	Matt 3.17 (A); 17.5 (A); Mark 1.11 (A); 9.7 (A); Luke 3.22 (A); 9.35 (A); Acts 13.33; Heb 1.5a; 5.5; 2 Peter 1.17 (A)
2.8-9	Rev 2.26-27 (A)
4.4 (4.5)	Eph 4.26 (A)
5.10 (5.9)	Rom 3.13-18
6.9 (6.8)	Matt 7.23 (A); Luke 13.27 (A)
8.3 (8.2)	Matt 21.26
8.4-6 (8.5-7)	Heb 2.6-8
8.6 (8.7)	1 Cor 15.27 (P); Eph 1.22 (A)
9.8 (9.9)	Acts 17.31 (A)
9.28 (10.7)	Rom 3.13-18

13.1,2,3 (14.1,2,3)	Rom 3.10-18
15.8-11 (16.8-11)	Acts 2.25-28
15.10 (16.10)	Acts 2.27,31 (P); 13.35
18.5 (19.4)	Rom 10.18
17.50 (18.49)	Rom 15.9
21.2 (22.1)	Matt 27.46; Mark 15.34
21.19 (22.18)	Matt 27.35 (A); Mark 15.24 (A); Luke 23.34 (A); John 19.24
21.23 (22.22)	Heb 2.12
23.1 (24.1)	1 Cor 10.26
31.1-2a (32.1-2a)	Rom 4.7-8
30.6 (31.5)	Luke 23.46 (A)
33.9 (34.8)	1 Peter 2.3 (A)
33.13-17 (34.12-16)	1 Peter 3.10-12
33.21 (34.20)	John 19.36
35.2 (36.1)	Rom 3.13-18
34.19 (35.19)	John 15.25
36.11 (37.11)	Matt 5.5 (A)
39.7-9 (40.6-8)	Heb 10.5-7,8,9,10
40.10 (41.9)	John 13.18
43.23 (44.22)	Rom 8.36
44.7-8 (45.6-7)	Heb 1.8-9
47.3 (48.2)	Matt 5.34-35 (A)
50.6 (51.4)	Rom 3.4
54.23 (55.22)	1 Peter 5.7 (A)
61.13 (62.12)	Matt 16.27 (A); Rom 2.6 (A); 2 Tim 4.14 (A)
66.3 (67.2)	Acts 28.28 (A)
67.19 (68.18)	Eph 4.8
68.5 (69.4)	John 15.25

68.10 (69.9)	John 2.17; Rom 15.3
68.22 (69.21)	Matt 27.48 (A); Mark 15.36 (A); John 19.28-29 (A)
68.23-24 (69.22-23)	Rom 11.9-10
68.26 (69.25)	Acts 1.20a
77.2 (78.2)	Matt 13.35
77.24 (78.28)	John 6.31 (P)
78.6 (79.6)	2 Thess 1.8 (A)
81.6 (82.6)	John 10.34
88.4-5 (89.3-4)	Acts 2.30 (P)
88.21 (89.20)	Acts 13.32 (P)
89.4 (90.4)	2 Peter 3.8 (A)
90.11-12 (91.11-12)	Mark 4.6; Luke 4.10-11
93.11 (94.11)	1 Cor 3.20
93.14 (94.14)	Rom 11.2 (A)
94.7-8 (95.7-8)	Heb 3.7-8a,15; 4.7
94.7-11 (95.7-11)	Heb 3.7-11
94.11 (95.11)	Heb 3.11,18; 4.3,4,5,10 (A)
96.13 (95.13)	Acts 17.31 (A)
97.9 (98.9)	Acts 17.31 (A)
101.26-28 (102.25-27)	Heb 1.10-12
102.8 (103.8)	James 5.11 (A)
102.17 (103.17)	Luke 1.50 (A)
103.4 (104.4)	Heb 1.7
108.8 (109.8)	Acts 1.20b
109.1 (110.1)	Matt 22.44; 26.64 (A); Mark 12.36; 14.62 (A); 16.19 (A); Luke 20.42-43; 22.69 (A); Acts 2.34-35; 1 Cor 15.25 (A);

	Eph 1.20,22 (A); Col 3.1 (A); Heb 1.3 (A); 13; 8.1 (A); 10.12-13 (A); 12.2 (A)
109.4 (110.4)	Heb 5.6; 7.17,21
111.9 (112.9)	2 Cor 9.9
113.12-15 (115.4-7)	Rev 9.20 (A)
115.1 (116.10)	2 Cor 4.13
116.1 (117.1)	Rom 15.11
117.6 (118.6)	Heb 13.6
117.22-23 (118.22-23)	Matt 21.42; Mark 12.10-11; Luke 20.17; Acts 4.11; 1 Peter 2.7
117.25-26 (118.25-26)	Matt 21.9 (A), 23.39 (A); Mark 11.9-10 (A); Luke 13.35 (A); 19.38 (A); John 12.13
117.26 (118.26)	Matt 21.9 (A); 23.39 (A); Luke 13.35b (A); 19.38 (A)
129.8 (130.8)	Titus 2.14 (A)
131.11 (132.11)	Acts 2.30 (P)
134.14 (135.14)	Heb 10.30b
134.15-17 (135.15-17)	Rev 9.20 (A)
139.4 (140.3)	Rom 3.10-18
142.2 (143.2)	Rom 3.20 (A); Gal 2.16 (A)
145.6 (146.6)	Acts 4.24 (A); 14.15 (A); Rev 10.6 (A); 14.7 (A)

PROVERBS

3.4	Rom 12.17 (P); 2 Cor 8.21 (P)
3.11-12	Heb 12.5-6
3.12	Rev 3.19 (A)
3.34	1 Peter 5.5; James 4.6

4.26	Heb 12.12-13 (A)	22.22	Rev 3.7 (A)
10.12	1 Peter 4.8 (A)	24.17	Luke 21.34-35 (A)
11.31	1 Peter 4.18 (A)	25.8	1 Cor 15.54
22.8	2 Cor 9.7 (A)	26.11	Heb 10.27 (A)
23.31	Eph 5.18 (A)	27.9	Rom 11.26-27
24.12	Matt 16.27; Rom 2.6 (A); 2 Tim 4.14 (A)	28.11-12	1 Cor 14.21
		28.16	Rom 9.33 (P); 10.11; 1 Peter 2.6
25.21-22	Rom 12.20	29.10	Rom 11.8
26.11	2 Peter 2.22	29.13	Matt 15.8-9; Mark 7.6-7; Col 2.22 (A)
	ISAIAH	29.14	1 Cor 1.19
1.9	Rom 9.29	29.16	Rom 9.20 (A)
2.19,20,21	2 Thess 1.9 (A)	35.3	Heb 12.12-13 (A)
5.1-2	Matt 21.33 (A); Mark 12.1 (A); Luke 20.9 (A)	35.5-6	Luke 4.18; 7.22 (A)
		40.3	Matt 3.3; Mark 1.3; Luke 3.4; John 1.23
5.9	James 5.4 (A)		
6.3	Rev 4.8 (A)	40.3-5	Luke 3.4-6
6.9	Luke 8.10 (A)	40.6-7	James 1.10-11 (A); 1 Peter 1.24-25
6.9-10	Matt 13.14-15; Mark 4.12; Acts 28.26-27		
		40.6-8	1 Peter 1.24-25
6.10	John 12.40 (P)	40.9	John 12.15
7.14	Matt 1.23	40.13	Rom 11.34; 1 Cor 2.16
8.12-13	1 Peter 3.14-15 (A)	41.8	James 2.23b (A)
8.14 (MT)	Rom 9.33,10.11; Heb 2.13b; 1 Peter 2.8	41.8-9	Heb 2.16a (A)
		42.1	Matt 3.17 (A); 17.5 (A); Mark 1.11 (A); 9.7; Luke 3.22; 9.35 (A); 2 Peter 1.17 (A)
8.17	Heb 2.13a		
8.18	Heb 2.13b		
9.1-2	Matt 4.15-16	42.1-3	Matt 12.18-21
9.2	Matt 4.16 (A); Luke 1.79 (A)	42.4	Matt 12.21
10.22-23	Rom 9.27-28	43.6	2 Cor 6.18 (P)
11.2	1 Peter 4.14 (A)	43.20-21	1 Peter 2.9 (A)
11.4	Eph 6.17 (A); 2 Thess 2.8 (A)	44.28	Acts 13.22 (P)
11.5	Eph 6.14-15 (A)	45.9	Rom 9.20 (A)
11.10	Rom 15.12	45.23	Rom 14.11; Phps 2.10-11 (A)
14.13,15	Matt 11.23 (A); Luke 10.15 (A)	49.1	Gal 1.15 (A)
22.13	1 Cor 15.32	49.2 (MT)	Eph 6.17 (A)

49.6	Acts 13.47	66.14	John 16.22 (A)
49.8	2 Cor 6.2	66.15	2 Thess 1.8 (A)
49.18	Rom 14.11	66.2	2 Peter 3.13 (A)
52.5	Rom 2.24	66.24	Mark 9.48 (A)
52.7	Rom 10.15; Eph 2.17 (A); 6.14-15 (A)		
			JEREMIAH
52.11	2 Cor 6.17 (P)	1.5	Gal 1.15 (A)
52.15	Rom 15.21; 1 Cor 2.9	5.21	Mark 8.18 (A)
53.1	John 12.38; Rom 10.16	6.16	Matt 11.29 (A)
53.3	Acts 13.47	7.11	Matt 21.13b (A); Mark 11.17b (A); Luke 19.46b (A)
53.4	Matt 8.17		
53.4-6	1 Peter 2.24-25 (A)	9.24	1 Cor 1.31; 2 Cor 10.17
53.7-8	Acts 8.32-33	10.25	2 Thess 1.8 (A)
53.9	1 Peter 2.22 (A)	18.16	Rom 9.21 (A)
53.12	Luke 22.37; Heb 9.28 (A); 1 Peter 2.24-25 (A)	22.5	Matt 23.38 (A); Luke 13.35a (A)
		31.15	Matt 2.18
54.1	Gal 4.27	31.33-34	John 6.45; Rom 11.26-27
54.13	John 6.45	38.31-34	Heb 8.8-12
55.3	Acts 13.34	(31.31-34)	
56.7b	Matt 21.13a; Mark 11.17a; Luke 19.46a	38.33,34	Heb 8.10,12; 10.16
		(31.33,34)	
57.19	Eph 2.17 (A)	51.45	2 Cor 6.17 (P)
58.6	Matt 11.5; Luke 4.18-19		
59.7-8	Rom 3.13-18		**EZEKIEL**
59.17 (MT)	Eph 6.14-15 (A), 17 (A); 1 Thess 5.8 (A)	12.2	Mark 8.18 (A)
		20.34,41	2 Cor 6.17 (P)
59.20-21	Rom 11.26-27	28.2	2 Thess 2.4 (A)
61.1	Matt 11.5 (A); Luke 7.22 (A)	34.5	Mark 6.34 (A)
61.1-2	Luke 4.18-19	37.23	Titus 2.14 (A)
62.11	Matt 21.5; John 12.15	37.27	2 Cor 6.16 (P)
64.4	1 Cor 2.9		
65.1	Rom 10.20		**DANIEL**
65.2	Rom 10.21	5.23	Rev 9.20 (A)
65.17	2 Peter 3.13 (A)	7.13	Matt 24.30b (A); 26.64 (A); Mark 12.36, 13.26 (A); 14.62 (A); Luke 21.27, 27 (A); Rev
66.1	Matt 5.34-35 (A)		
66.2-1	Acts 7.49-50		

Appendix

1.7a (A)

7.21	Rev 13.7 (A)
11.31	Matt 24.15 (A); Mark 13.14 (A)
11.36	2 Thess 2.4 (A)
12.11	Matt 24.15 (A); Mark 13.14 (A)

HOSEA

1.6,9	1 Peter 2.10 (A)
1.10a	Rom 9.27-28
2.1 (1.10)	Rom 9.26
2.1,23	1 Peter 2.10 (A)
2.23	Rom 9.25
6.5	Eph 6.17 (A)
6.6	Matt 9.13; 12.7
10.8	Luke 23.30 (A); Rev 6.16 (A)
11.1	Matt 2.15
13.14	1 Cor 15.55

JOEL

3.1-5	Acts 2.27-21
3.5	Acts 2.21; Rom 10.13
3.13	Mark 4.29 (A)

AMOS

5.25-27	Acts 7.42-43
9.11-12	Acts 15.16-18

JONAH

1.17	Matt 12.40 (A)
5.2	Matt 2.6
7.6	Luke 12.53 (A)

MICAH

5.2	Matt 2.6; John 7.42 (P)
7.6	Matt 10.35-36 (A); Luke 12.53 (A)

NAHUM

1.15	Rom 10.15; Eph 6.15

HABAKKUK

1.5	Acts 13.41
2.3-4	Heb 10.37-38
2.4	Rom 1.17; Gal 3.11; Heb 10.35

HAGGAI

2.6	Heb 12.26

ZECHARIAH

3.2	Jude 9
8.16	Eph 4.25 (A)
9.9	Matt 21.5; John 12.15
11.12	Matt 26.15 (A)
11.12-13	Matt 27.9-10
12.10	John 19.37; Rev 1.76b (A)
13.7	Matt 26.31; Mark 14.27

MALACHI

1.2-3	Rom 9.13
3.1	Matt 3.3 (A); 11.10; Mark 1.2-3; Luke 1.76 (A); 7.27
4.5-6	Luke 1.17 (A)

PSEUDEPIGRAPHA

1 ENOCH

1.9; 5.4; 60.8	Jude 14-15

ISBN 082670031-4